'This refreshing book left me wan~~t~~ ~~ing to put my~~ newfound knowledge to the test by proactively embracing the next difficult conversation! Written in a creative and dynamic way, *Curly Conversations for Teams* captures the reader's attention with a combination of comparative storytelling, cognitive insights and smart ideas to help us tap into our emotional and adaptable intelligence. It's super practical which means change agent leaders can easily and intuitively extract value to support their teams through change and disruption. There has never been a more perfect time to embrace Curly Conversations than right now.'

Ricki Vinci, Chief Financial Officer & Company Secretary,
Safe Steps

'The ability to have Curly Conversations is necessary for all high-performing teams. Kate's practical, step-by-step approach is a pragmatic method of introducing these into a team, in a respectful, professional and non-threatening way. The practical guides at the back of the book cover most, if not all, of the scenarios any team leader or manager is likely to encounter. A great addition to any leader's handbook!'

Geoff Purcell, Chief Technology Officer
Melbourne Water

'Having a disruptive conversation with your team is not an art form – it requires courage, discipline and practice. Now, thanks to Kate Christiansen, there is also a reliable framework to make these conversations predictable, frequent and successful. Using memorable concepts and inspiring stories, Kate guides us on ways to create a safe environment for teams to ask bold questions, challenge the status quo and create strategies to address the disruption they face.'

Anneliese Rhodes, Director Customer Experience
Cisco Systems - EMEAR

'This book is a wonderful, practical guide for leaders and their teams at a time where change, discomfort and disruption are accelerating at a pace few of us have ever experienced. *Curly Conversations for Teams* makes the unknown less lonely and scary. It will challenge your thinking and provide the confidence every leader needs to step into uncertainty, deliver results and create true strategic value.'

Andy McKechnie, Chief Retail Banking Officer
Al Masraf Bank, UAE

'Disruption has accelerated changes to how we work and added new challenges for all of us to understand and negotiate. In *Curly Conversations for Teams*, Kate offers a guide to deal with the "difficult" conversations that teams need to have. This book provides leaders with positive and productive ways to deliver team-based results, while building strong teamwork cultures.'

Phil Tuckett, Global Operations Leader
Suez - Upstream Oil and Gas

'I love this book! It is fresh, delightfully easy to read and incredibly practical. *Curly Conversations for Teams* is THE playbook for leaders who want support in a world of change and disruption. Let Kate guide you to inspire your team to embrace conundrums and truly learn to think differently.'

Amanda Lutvey, Communication &
Engagement Specialist
Maven Dental Group

'*Curly Conversations for Teams* is an excellent resource filled with practical solutions, built from lived experiences, to challenges universally faced by teams responding to disruption.'

Carolyn Noumertzis, Chief Human Resources Officer

'Kate Christiansen has a truly unique way of inspiring and motivating teams to take big steps, tackle big questions and shift their thinking into the realm of possibility.'

Beau Vigushin, Executive Director Customer Experience
Art Centre Melbourne

Curly Conversations for Teams is a powerful, engaging and wonderful book. Kate has an incredible ability to skilfully weave her considerable insights and real-life stories into a thought provoking, practical and structured toolkit. A must read for any leader and their team operating in today's constantly changing and disrupted environment, who wishes to have Curly Conversations with confidence.'

Emma Dyer, Human Resources Manager
Licella Group

Curly Conversations for Teams is a breath of fresh air for disrupted leaders and teams. If you want to have energising team conversations that overcome the hidden elements that stifle collaboration, performance, development and trust - read this book!'

Melinda Benbow, Supply Planning Manager
The Body Shop

About the author

Kate Christiansen is Australia's leading expert on Curly Conversations.

She is an award-winning author, mentor and educator who has spent 25 years tackling curly conundrums across the world.

Kate knows first-hand what it feels like to be faced with seemingly impossible questions and high-stakes expectations. Questions like:

- How do we provide quality healthcare in a market where we can't trust the doctors and the medications are fake?

- How do we respond to global regulations that don't make any sense?

- How do we get 60,000 people excited about the most boring topic in the world?

- How do we make our global business truly customer-centric?

- How do we overcome silos when it's been this way for 30 years?

Kate shares her compassion, experience and deep insight with leaders and teams, through mentoring and education programs. Her unique ability to unpack the art and science behind Curly Conversations enables her clients to embrace uncertainty and step into the unknown with confidence.

Kate's first book, The Thrive Cycle: Unlock the Adaptive Organisation Within, was awarded an Axiom Business Book Medal in 2017.

Curly Conversations

FOR TEAMS

DIVE INTO DISCOMFORT
DARE TO DO THINGS DIFFERENTLY
DELIVER DESPITE DISRUPTION

KATE CHRISTIANSEN

Published by Handson Media, Melbourne.

First Published in Australia 2021

Copyright © 2021 100% Care Pty Ltd

A catalogue record for this work is available from the National Library of Australia

All rights reserved. No part of this publication may be reproduced stored in a retrieval system, or transmitted, in any form or by any means without prior written consent of the copyright owner, nor be otherwise circulated in any form of binding or cover other than that in which it is published and without a similar condition being imposed on the subsequent purchaser.

Curly Conversations for Teams: Dive into discomfort, Dare to do things differently, Deliver despite disruption.

Written by Kate Christiansen
ISBN: 978-0-9944751-1-4

Cover design – TK Palad
Internal design and type-setting – Hammad Khalid
1st round editing – Matt Ralph
2nd round editing – Gabrielle Prior

Curly Conversations™; Curly Conversation Starters™; including contents, formats and graphic representations are trademarks of 100% Care Pty Ltd. This book may not be incorporated into or used as part of any commercial program without the express written permission of the copyright owner.

DISCLAIMER

All care has been taken in the preparation of the information herein, but no responsibility can be accepted by the publisher or author for any damages resulting from the misinterpretation of the work. All contact details given in this book were current at the time of publication but are subject to change. The advice given in this book is based upon the experience of individuals. The author and publisher shall not be responsible for any person with regard to any loss or damage caused directly, or indirectly by the information in this book.

For the leaders who step into disruption without having all the answers and with the courage and humility to admit it.

CONTENTS

Introduction

Progress is impossible without change; and those who cannot change their minds, cannot change anything.

George Bernard-Shaw

The power of perspective

I have naturally curly hair.

In my experience, people with hair like mine tend to fall into one of three categories. Those who love it, those who live with it and those who loathe it. I've spent most of my life somewhere between living with it and loathing it.

When I was in primary school, I looked enviously at all the girls with sleek, straight hair wishing my hair could look that neat. In my teens and early twenties I tried plenty of different strategies to make this wish come true.

I cut my hair off so there wasn't enough hair for the curls to form. I ironed it with my mother's iron. I used a chemical straightener that was so strong that my hair bent at right angles and broke off.

Only decades later did I realise that it wasn't my hair that was the problem, it was my thinking. Somehow, I had set up a hair hierarchy with straight hair at the top and curly hair underneath it. As a result, according to my hierarchy, the best version of curly hair was straight hair.

Then, one day it occurred to me.

What if I stopped trying to make my curly hair into straight hair? What if, instead of seeing one as being better than the other, they were equal, just different? And, what if when defining a great hairstyle, I emphasised the unique characteristics of curly hair and drew on its strengths, rather than fighting against them.

Now, as you read this you may be thinking "Seriously? It took her decades to work this out?"

It's obvious, right?

Just as common sense isn't always common, the obvious only becomes obvious after someone has pointed it out.

Anyway, this new way of thinking gave me a different perspective and a fresh way to relate to my hair. I started to accept and value what I had instead of fighting against it and wishing it was something else. I looked for ways to emphasise my curls, and instead of resenting the unpredictable nature of the hair, I started to appreciate the energy that was embedded within its spring-like shape.

But what does any of this have to do with conversations in teams?

Perhaps more than one might at first expect.

The 'too hard' basket

A team conversation is a uniquely human tool that enables two or more people to understand a challenge, exchange ideas, explore options and then address it, even if that challenge is yet to occur. Conversations enable us to use language to think together, work together and connect emotionally with each other.

In teams, some conversations are harder than others. They make us feel less comfortable, make our brains work much harder and leave us feeling confused and frustrated. This is particularly so during times of disruption.

This book is about these conversations: the so-called *difficult* ones that are the inevitable consequences of disruption. The ones that many teams struggle with, and that often fall into the 'too hard' basket. These difficult conversations lead to confusion, lack of alignment and compromised outcomes.

But let's pause here for a second.

- *When I talk about a difficult team conversation, what do you think of?*

- *What happens in your team when it needs to have one of these conversations?*

Alright. Now let's take this thinking a little deeper.

- *When you think about a difficult team conversation, what are you comparing it to?*

When I ask this question in leadership sessions, participants usually answer that they are comparing it to a conversation that is *not difficult.*

But what does that mean?

Participants usually answer that it's a conversation that is straightforward. It is one in which they feel comfortable, their brains don't need to work too hard and where they leave the conversation feeling clear and ready to take action.

I've spent several decades leading and having team conversations that weren't straightforward. I've done so in some of the most disrupted and complex environments in the world.

As a corporate leader and later as a mentor and educator, I've learnt that the conversations that we call *difficult* are not inherently so. We make them difficult by the way we think and respond in uncertain situations.

When we think of a conversation as being difficult, we fall into the same trap that I fell into when thinking about my curly hair.

We put straightforward conversations and those that aren't straightforward on a single hierarchy in our heads. Straightforward team conversations are at the top. They are easier, and therefore the ones that we want to have. Then, somewhere way down the hierarchy are the team conversations that aren't straightforward. We think of these as difficult conversations and they are the ones that we'd prefer *not* to have.

We need a new way

As leaders, and I would argue as human beings, we face a growing and important challenge.

Straightforward situations lend themselves to straightforward, easy conversations. However, thanks to disruption, many of the situations that used to be straightforward are no longer so. That's because disruption shifts our environment and consequently dislodges the assumptions upon which straightforward conversations rely. It's like cooking in your kitchen when someone else has dried the dishes and put them away in the wrong place. It makes a previously straightforward task like boiling an egg, less straightforward because the things you need are no longer where you expect them to be.

In addition, a new breed of 'situation' is emerging. It's the kind that is unprecedented and completely different to anything else we've experienced in the past.

But what does this mean and why is it a problem? Three reasons.

Firstly, there is a *decreasing* need for the straightforward conversations that we like and find easy. Secondly, there is an *increasing* need to have the so-called difficult conversations that we don't like and find hard. Finally, the unprecedented situations that make the world more complex also make the difficult conversations more difficult. This amplifies the effects of the other two reasons.

All of the leaders I work with face the consequences of these trends every day. Most find the experience relentless, frustrating and exhausting. Many question how long they can continue with the way things are.

I know from experience that being a leader is challenging. Now it is even more so, as expectations continue to increase while certainty decreases. The ways of the past no longer support leaders in the present or into the future. It's one of the reasons that we need a better and easier way to lead through disruption.

However, there is an even bigger, yet hidden, challenge. It is the catalyst behind this book and the driver behind the passion and energy I put into the work I do.

Like straight and curly hair, straightforward and difficult conversations are fundamentally different to each other. However, many teams treat these conversations as though they are the same. More specifically, they treat all conversations as though they are straightforward.

But why does this happen?

When I ask this question of leaders, many say that it is a matter of practicality. When they are busy 'doing the work', leaders want conversations to be quick, easy and deliver the desired result.

In my experience, this answer is underpinned by an unspoken belief. Namely, that conversations which are *not* straightforward are by definition, slow and difficult, and they rarely deliver the desired result.

As one leader described it, "Difficult team conversations will always be difficult and there is nothing that anyone can do about it."

I disagree.

That's why this book sets out to inspire hope and to empower leaders and their teams who increasingly face waves of disruption on a daily basis. It does so by providing a solution: the Curly Conversation.

What is a Curly Conversation?

A Curly Conversation enables any team to respond positively to a situation that is not straightforward. Instead of pre-judging a situation as *difficult*, it is accepted as merely being *different*. Just like me and my curly hair, this shift in thinking creates a positive new lens through which teams can relate and respond to disruption. This sets them up to succeed from the very start.

Curly conversations are different in four key ways.

They happen by design, not by default

A straightforward conversation does not usually need to be planned or designed. That's because it follows a familiar, well-worn path. In a disrupted environment however, there is no path to follow, which is why a Curly Conversation needs to be designed. This defines a path for the conversation to follow and makes it feel easier.

For this reason, a Curly Conversation is a carefully designed and open discussion. It creates a safe environment in which participants can take risks and think complex challenges through, together.

They are flexible, yet controlled

Curly Conversations twist and turn in a controlled way, working with the ragged nature of a disrupted environment. They provide a framework to enable teams to navigate uncertainty together in a calm and confident way. When doing so, they build a sense of connection between team members. This ensures that when there is a change of direction, everyone moves together.

They are holistic and keep human instincts in check

Curly Conversations pay equal attention to the people, the path and the outcome. They enable your team to sit more comfortably with the tension that is created when team members want an answer but don't yet know what it is. This reduces the risk of team members prematurely leaping to obvious, but potentially wrong, solutions.

They are energising, not exhausting

A Curly Conversation has the power to turn a fractious and frustrating team discussion into one that is fun and focused. That's because when people experience a great Curly Conversation, they become deeply engaged in the challenge and lose track of time. Focus shifts away from the petty small issues that can create such a distraction, and instead, people focus on the outcome.

If you'd like to have more of this kind of conversation in your team, this book is the springboard that will get you on your way.

You are not alone

Leadership can be lonely. This is especially so when you are out of your comfort zone and trying to lead through a fog of uncertainty.

The good news is that it doesn't have to be this way. This book is like having a mentor in your pocket. Someone who understands first-hand what it's like, and who can help you in the moment to engage and galvanise your team to achieve incredible results.

Curly Conversations for Teams is a practical introduction and resource designed to be shared and used with your team. Together you will learn:

- how to relate differently to disruption and have a shared language that enables your team to talk about it
- why conversations that are not straightforward become difficult
- how to work out what kind of conversation your team needs to have
- what kinds of conversations your team is having today
- the stages involved in developing Curly Conversation capability
- how to have a Curly Conversation as a team

Part 1 provides the essential context. It looks at the concept of disruption and how it can affect a team and its ability to do its job. We'll explore how our comfort zone influences our ability to think through complex situations. With this knowledge, we can make disruption and the changes it triggers significantly less scary.

In Part 2 we discuss the different types of conversations that teams have when they are in their discomfort zone. You'll plot your team on the Conversation Continuum and learn the three critical factors behind great Curly Conversations. You'll also be introduced to a three-stage roadmap showing how to increase the conversational capability of your team.

Parts 3 and 4 are the practical toolkit. They introduce a pre-designed conversation framework called a Curly Conversation Starter. There are 15 of these ready-to-use conversations that you can try out straight away. They cover topics like trust, setting the right priorities, taking risks, building alignment while also allowing you and your team to develop Curly Conversation skills.

I'm really excited to share *Curly Conversations for Teams* with you and I'm looking forward to hearing how you go.

You'll find more tools, insights and support at **www.curlyconversations.com**.

For now, however, it's time to get curly and curious.

Kate Christiansen

E: **hello@katechristiansen.com.au**

HOW SHOULD WE RESPOND TO THE UN-
HOW DO WE BUILD TRUST? EXPECTED?
HOW DO WHO DO WE THINK DIFFERENTLY?
ENGAGE ARE WE KEEPING HOW DO WE GET ON THE
OUR PEOPLE HOW DO OUR PROMISES? SAME PAGE?
COULD WE CHALLENGE OLD HABITS?
WE MAKE HOW DO WE CONNECT BETTER
BETTER WITH EACH OTHER TO INTEGRITY?
CHOICES WHAT DOES IT MEAN TO HAVE INTEGRITY?
DO WE HAVE DO WE LEARN FROM OUR MISTAKES?
DO WE HAVE IS OUR STRATEGY DOING ITS JOB?
THE RIGHT HOW DO WE HARNESS THE POWER
PRIORITIES SELF DISCIPLINE OF PURPOSE
DO WE TAKE DO WE SEIZE ENOUGH?
THE RIGHT RISKS? OUR OPPORTUNITIES?

PART 1:

A HUMAN
APPROACH

The parrot
in the pipe

Every weekday morning, I'm woken up by my clock radio blaring the latest news. When the news ends, that's my cue to get out of bed and start my morning routine. But the other day I was feeling a bit lazy, so I lay in bed a little longer. That is when the following story came on[1].

It was the early hours of a winter's morning in Melbourne when Sewer Contract Manager James Mitchell and his team were called out to fix a blocked pipe.

They closed off the road, opened up the manhole and put the inspection camera down the sewer pipe to see what was causing the blockage. The blocked pipe was ten metres (33 feet) below the road's surface along a smaller, horizontal branch pipe.

When the camera had progressed sixty metres (197 feet) along the branch pipe, James heard a commotion coming from the team's van. He popped his head inside and saw a couple of team members gathered around the camera's video monitor.

They couldn't believe their eyes.

There, sitting on a rock in the middle of the pipe was a parrot, specifically, a galah. The team were used to finding lots of different obstacles in the sewer pipes, but this was their first parrot.

The camera was mounted on a remote-controlled trolley. As this approached the parrot, the bird calmly stepped to one side and allowed the camera to continue down the pipe to the blocked area. However, a little further along, James and his team encountered an issue.

The sides of the pipe were too slippery for the camera trolley to gain traction. Unfortunately, the only way for the maintenance team to finish the job was to clean the pipe. This involved inserting a high-pressure hose and blasting the area with water.

The parrot's prospects were looking a little grim.

On the surface, the maintenance team frantically searched for different options, but none ended happily for the parrot. Meanwhile, time was ticking. Peak hour traffic was due to start and the road needed to be re-opened.

The team concluded that they had no alternative but to blast the pipe with water. They started to bring the camera back down the pipe.

As James describes it, "That's when something freaky happened." As the camera trolley approached the parrot, the bird hopped onto the back as if to hitch a ride.

Travelling at a brisk walking pace, the parrot stayed on the back of the trolley for the full sixty metre ride back to the opening of the branch pipe. In the van, the maintenance team could see the parrot on the video monitor, and it could be heard chirping all the way.

Once the parrot and camera reached the main pipe, James and his team faced another dilemma.

How could they retrieve the parrot ten metres down without scaring it back up the pipe?

They looked at what was available in the van. Eventually they strapped a few grappling hooks together and created a wobbly, extra-long pole. The team lowered it down from the top of the manhole with the parrot watching intently. As the pole reached the parrot, the bird simply stepped onto the hook. It rode on it all the way to James and his waiting team on the surface. Apart from being very dirty, the parrot seemed to be in good health, so James put it up in a nearby tree and the crew continued to clear the pipe and carry on their way.

Getting jobs done

The contractors working on the sewer pipe were trying to get a job done: clear the blockage before peak-hour traffic arrived.

While most of us don't fix sewer pipes for a living, we too spend our waking hours trying to get important jobs done.

When we're at school, we focus on jobs like making friends, getting good grades or having a good time. As adults we focus on jobs like earning a living, giving our kids an education, putting dinner on the table, having positive relationships, being healthy, having a successful career and so on.

At work, we also spend a significant amount of time getting work jobs done. For example, building or maintaining a high-performing team, achieving sales targets or having satisfied customers, to name just a few.

Our jobs come in different sizes and have different priorities. Some are more fun or more interesting than others. However, all have the same objective. That is, to create a shift from a less desirable current state to a more desirable future state.

In other words, jobs are how we get from [A] to [B], where [A] is where we *are*, and [B] is where we *want* to be. Importantly, the way we frame the job in our heads, determines the steps and tasks that we attempt to complete when getting that job done.

For the people working on the sewer pipe, [A] was having a pipe that was blocked, and [B] was having a pipe that was unblocked. The team's job was to unblock the pipe before peak-hour traffic started.

Figure 1 - The objective of every job is to get from A to B.

A ⟶ B

Where we
are

Where we
want to be

Many of the jobs that we do in teams are routine or operational. These jobs are straightforward. They are well-known, form predictable patterns and we have significant experience doing them. The maintenance team working on the blocked pipe had 30-years of experience between them.

For them, unblocking a sewer pipe was a routine job.

When our environment is stable, routine jobs collectively form the basis of a team's function. Ultimately, the jobs we do create the outcomes we want, so our team can fulfil its purpose.

Figure 2 - Jobs deliver outcomes that fulfil purpose

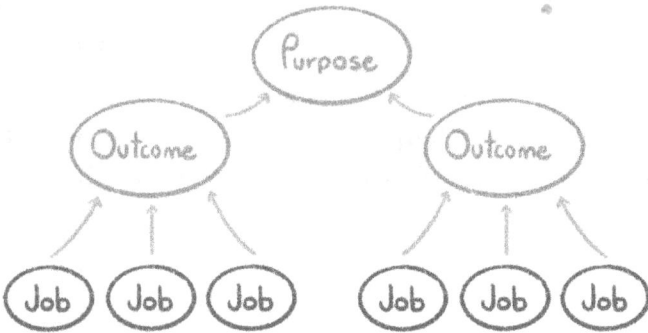

Some examples of these jobs include:

- Delivering products and services
- Responding to customer enquiries
- Producing finance reports
- Achieving sales targets
- Recruiting and developing employees
- Purchasing equipment
- Delivering projects
- Advertising

In an ideal world, getting from [A] to [B] would be straightforward. Everything would go according to plan; nothing would get in our way and the journey from [A] to [B] would be straightforward and friction-free.

However, as the sewerage workers discovered, sometimes a job that should be straightforward, turns out not to be.

That pain in the 'but-so'

When disruption occurs and catapults obstacles onto our previously clear path, it creates a conundrum. That is, a confusing or difficult question that prevents us from being able to move forward as planned.

How do you know if you're caught in a conundrum?

Well, one way is to listen to the way that you or others describe the situation. You will often find that you put the words 'but' and 'so' in the middle of the sentence. As you can see below, these two words divide conundrums into three parts: the job we were attempting to complete, the disruption that got in the way, and the consequence of the disruption.

Examples of common Conundrums

Job to be done		Disruption		Consequence
I was **driving to work**	BUT	my usual route was blocked off	SO	I ended up being 15 minutes late
We were **buying a house**	BUT	the seller took a higher bid from someone else	SO	now we're going to house auctions all weekend
I moved to a new country to **take up my dream job**	BUT	the boss turned out to be a nightmare	SO	I came home 6 months early

Conundrums are often experienced by teams. Some of these examples may sound familiar:

- We have developed a new product *BUT* no one wants to buy it *SO* we're going to miss our sales target

- We need to have strong cashflow *BUT* we've just lost a contract with our biggest customer *SO* we need to cut costs
- We had the budget to deliver a game-changing project *BUT* the money has been reallocated to something else *SO* we need to find a new solution
- We want to grow our business *BUT* agile competitors are taking our customers *SO* we need to transform our organisation.

The ability to describe a conundrum is one of the first steps in being able to confront it as a team.

Time to reflect

Let's try the 'But-So' framework out using a live example from your team.

- *What's the biggest conundrum that your team is facing right now?*
- *If you were to put it into the 'but-so' framework above, how would you describe it?*

It's worth taking some time to think about this now because we're going to refer back to this example a couple of times later in the book.

Before we continue, there is an important point to raise.

When reading a book, especially one that has been written to be used as well as read, it's natural to want to get to the practical stuff as quickly as possible. In fact, I know plenty of leaders who would pick up this book and go straight to the toolkit in Parts 3 and 4.

If this has crossed your mind, that's okay. Our impetus for action is powerful and is frequently reinforced at work. I mean, when was the last time you were rewarded for *thinking* rather than *taking action* and *getting the work done?*

Curly Conversations aren't just about *doing* things differently, they are about *thinking* differently. To do this, we need to learn to pause and keep our addiction to action in check.

Stay with me for the next few chapters and I'll show you how to make thinking easier and more productive. I'll help you to understand disruption and the way it impacts you and your team. And, I'll share a practical framework that will enable your team members to think through a disruptive event together.

So, let's get cracking.

The two sides of disruption

Dr Julia Shaw is a psychological scientist at University College, London and an expert on the topic of 'evil'. More specifically, she looks at what factors lead to a person being considered evil, and how that impacts the conclusions we make about them and their behaviour.

In her book, *Making Evil: The Science Behind Humanity's Dark Side*, Dr Shaw makes the point that we often refer to someone as 'being evil' because we can't find a rational explanation for their abhorrent behaviour. She suggests that when we do this, it tricks our brain into believing we have an answer for why the event happened. This, in turn, switches off our curiosity and our desire to dig deeper and learn more.

Dr Shaw argues that as soon as we do this, we miss the opportunity to uncover the real reason for the behaviour and potentially prevent future events.

The term *disruption*, while less emotive than evil, is also used as a catch-all word to describe a situation that is seen as being unexplainable. This can lead to the assumption that the situation can't be understood, which in turn, drives fear and avoidance.

If we're going to calmly and confidently navigate disruption as a team, we need to be curious about it. We need to seek to understand it, and in a team this starts by being able to talk about it.

That's what this chapter will help you to do.

To start things off, I'd like you to imagine that you have a coin lying flat on a table in front of you. Like this coin, disruption has two sides.

Figure 3 - The two sides of disruption

Visible

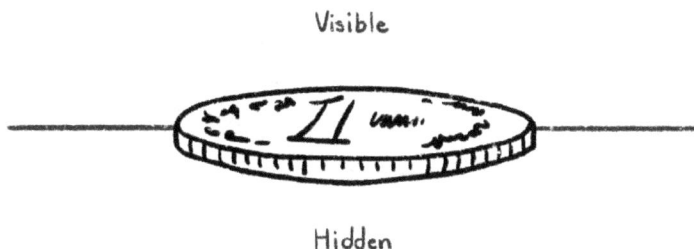

Hidden

The visible side

The first side of disruption is the *visible* side. This is the side of the coin facing up for all to see. This side is the practical one, the one that we can analyse and talk about. The visible side is the one that traditional problem-solving processes often focus on.

When the visible side of disruption impacts a job we're trying to do, it does so along three dimensions: The Context, the Path and the Direction.

Context – Was it expected?

The Context dimension concerns the extent to which the disruption was, or at least could have been, expected. This influences the degree to which the event surprises us, but also the extent to which our past experience will help us to address it.

For example, people living in the Philippines regularly experience typhoons around September and October each year. These events cause flooding, cut off power supplies and generally cause havoc. However, even though these natural disasters have a high impact, they are common, and therefore expected.

If a disruption is expected, we are better equipped to deal with it.

However, imagine if a typhoon hit Hobart, on the southern tip of Australia. This non-tropical location does not experience typhoons. So, it would be completely unexpected. Consequently, the people of Hobart would be less ready to deal with it.

Figure 4 - The visible side

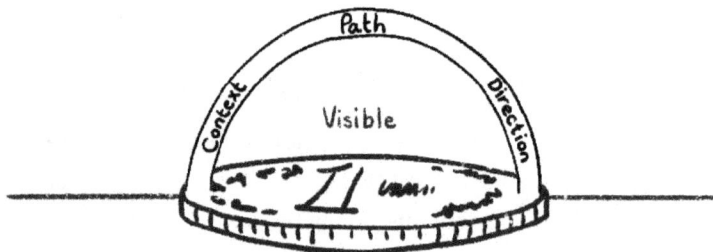

Path – Can I carry on doing what I was doing?

The Path is the expected sequence of steps that will get the job done. The Path dimension of disruption considers the degree to which these steps are still valid.

Sometimes they are valid. For example, when the disruption slows us down, but then we're able to get back on track and continue on the known path. Other times, disruption can make the path we were following irrelevant.

Direction – Can I keep going where I was going?

The Direction dimension relates to whether our planned path is still taking us to where we want to be (i.e., from [A] to [B]). Is it still going to deliver the outcome we want? Also, is the outcome that we previously wanted still the one we want now, even after the disruption has occurred?

✀

Let's take a look at these three dimensions in the context of the sewer story mentioned previously.

When the parrot appeared in the pipe, it disrupted the *Context* because parrots do not usually appear in sewer pipes. It was an anomaly, which even the most experienced sewerage worker was unlikely to have previously experienced. This made the situation more intense.

The parrot also disrupted the *Path*. The pipe was slippery and under normal circumstances, the team would have blasted it with water. However, because of the parrot, they were unable to apply their usual approach.

Also, the bird's appearance called into question the *Direction* the job was heading. The outcome was no longer just about unblocking the pipe. It was also about saving the bird.

Time to reflect

Okay. Let's come back to the example you identified for your team in the previous chapter.

- *How did the disruption impact the Context, the Path and the Direction?*
- *If you were to draw it like the journey from [A] to [B] above, what would it look like?*

By this point, you'll be starting to build up a picture of what happened, and specifically, what turned an otherwise routine job into a conundrum.

Now, let's lift up the coin and take a peek at what lies on the other side.

The hidden side

Most of us intuitively know that the hidden side of disruption exists because we feel it. It's the side that makes our hearts race and twists our stomachs in knots. It's our individual experience of disruption.

It's hidden because it can't be seen by anyone else and it varies between individuals. Consequently, the hidden side of disruption cannot be objectively analysed or summarised in the same way as the visible side.

Perhaps this is the reason that many problem-solving approaches prefer to ignore it.

Figure 5 - The hidden side

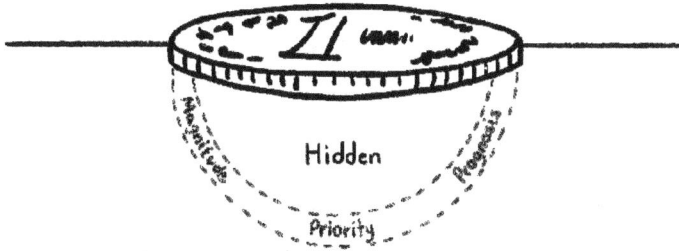

The hidden side of disruption is always viewed through the lens of our own experience.

The way we interpret what has happened and decide what it means to us, will be influenced by what we've experienced in the past. It will also be affected by other factors, like our personal preferences, beliefs and values.

The hidden side of disruption is the reason why, in a group of people who experience the same disruptive event, some feel deeply impacted, while others hardly notice it.

Like the visible side of disruption, the hidden side also has three dimensions. They are: the Magnitude, the Priority and the Prognosis.

Magnitude – How big is this disruption for me?

The Magnitude refers to how big we perceive the disruption to be. Where does it measure on our personal Richter Scale?

The perceived magnitude is influenced by several factors. For example, how close we are to the event and how different it is from our expectations of what is going to happen. Magnitude is also influenced by what has happened to us in the past.

For instance, if something similar, yet much bigger, occurred a year ago, we might see the current situation as relatively small. On the other hand, if we've never experienced this kind of situation before, we may see it as large.

Priority – How important is this job to me?

The second of these hidden dimensions is the Priority of the job. Do we personally care about it and care if the outcome is achieved? If the job is really important to us and an event puts it under threat, we are likely to feel more disrupted than if we care little about it.

In the parrot example, the job that was initially important was clearing the sewer pipe. However, as the events unfolded, the job became more complex because it also involved rescuing the parrot. While the parrot may not have been as important to the workers as their paid job, it was personally important enough to the team members and created disruption.

Prognosis – How will this disruption impact my future circumstances?

The third and final dimension on the hidden side of disruption is the Prognosis. This refers to our level of confidence that we can see to the other side beyond the disruptive event. The Prognosis is also influenced by whether we believe the event places us in a better or worse position than before.

✄

The visible side of disruption focuses on *what has happened*. The hidden side is concerned with *what it means to me*.

But why are the two sides of disruption so important, and why do they matter in teams?

When we understand how disruption works and how it affects not only what we're doing, but how we're feeling, it empowers our team to take action.

To truly understand disruption, we need to consider both the visible and hidden dimensions. We also need to consider each team member's experience of the situation.

But how do we consider so many different factors without becoming lost in complexity?

The Wheel of Disruption

Not all disruption is created equal.

In many ways, disruption is like an earthquake. Sometimes it causes a rumbling beneath our feet that is barely noticeable. Other times, it causes the walls to cave in, or the ground to drop away from beneath our feet.

When disruption causes a temporary rumbling, the job we're doing can often continue unimpeded.

If the disruption causes more of a tremor, it may interrupt our flow for a while. However, ultimately, we remain confident that we'll be able to bring things back on track and still get the job done.

Then, there are the times when disruption causes a seismic shift in the landscape around us. This can make us call into question not only whether the job will get done, but whether the job is even relevant, or important, anymore.

A tool that I use to understand whether I'm dealing with a rumble, a tremor or a seismic shift is *The Wheel of Disruption*. This takes the three dimensions from the visible side and the three from the hidden side and puts them together into one framework.

Figure 6 - The Wheel of Disruption

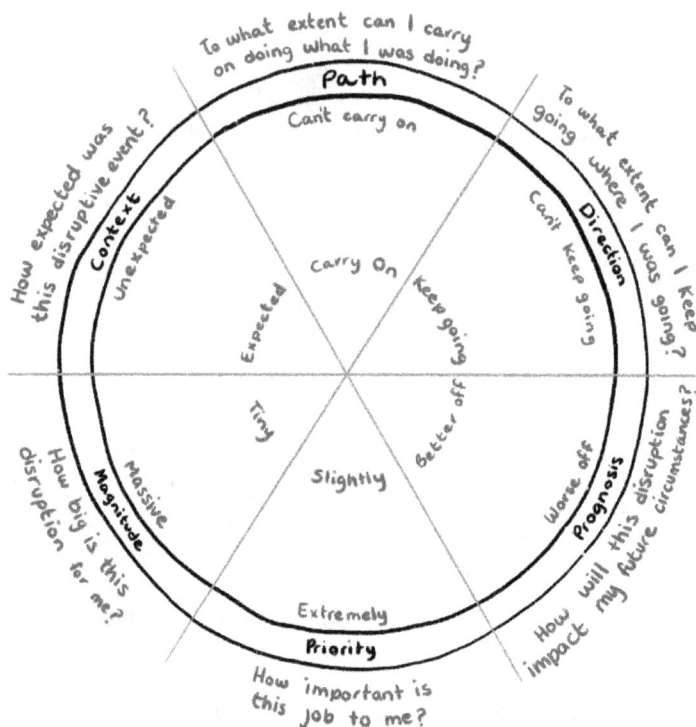

As you can see, each wedge has a question on the outer rim. And then, two potential answers are written in the wedge: one at the wide end near the rim, and the other towards the thin end, at the centre.

When we've experienced a rumbling, our answers tend to be very close to the centre. When disruption causes more of a tremor, our answers tend to fall around the middle of each wedge. And, if disruption has caused more of a seismic shift in our circumstances, then our answers tend to fall around the outer rim of the wheel.

Time to reflect

Let's bring this back to you again and test this out with the previous example from your team.

Using the questions around the outside of the Wheel of Disruption, plot where *you* were on each of the six dimensions. The diagram below gives you an example.

- *Was your experience more towards the centre or towards the rim of the wheel?*
- *Would you consider it to have been a rumble, a tremor or a seismic shift?*
- *How would other members of your team have rated it?*
- *If your rating was different to that of your team's, how might that have affected the conversation that occurred?*

Figure 7 – How to use the Wheel of Disruption

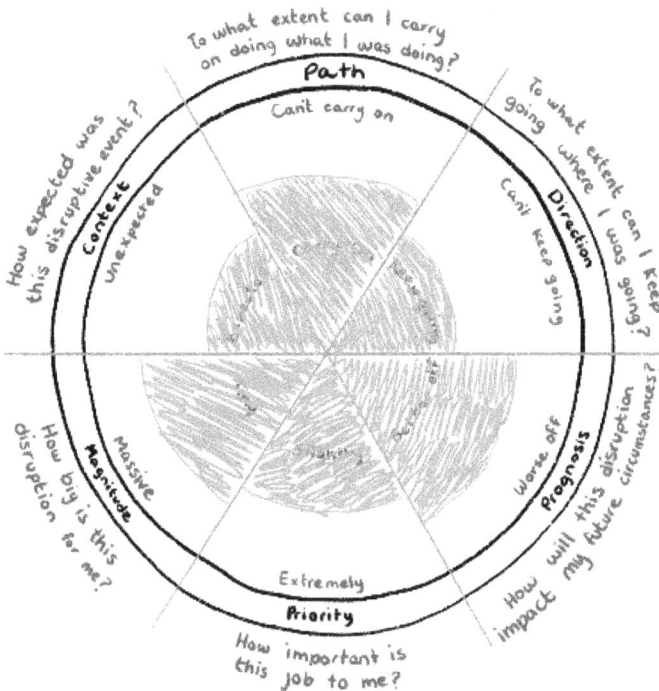

Humans, not robots

If you and I were robots, this book could pretty much stop here.

Once the Wheel of Disruption had helped us to understand what kind of disruption we were dealing with, we could simply plug it into some algorithmic model. This would have computed the response most likely to succeed (given all the possibilities and all the parameters) and told us exactly what to do, and how to do it.

But we're humans, not robots. Unfortunately, many traditional problem-solving approaches forget this. So, while they work in theory, they turn out to be less effective in practice.

I'm a practitioner, not a theorist. Two decades of experience has taught me that as humans, dealing with disruption and confronting the conundrums it creates requires more than a logical brain and intellectual calculations.

That's where this book comes in. It recognises that to succeed as leaders (and, I would argue, as humans) in a disrupted world, we need to account for the experience of disruption as much as the observable impact.

We need to connect how we think with how we feel and what we do. When our team has been disrupted, we need to do all of this, while also connecting with each other. And, we need to view the disruption through the lens of discomfort and the opportunities it creates.

Finally, we need a way to not only accept or deal with the discomfort of disruption, we need a way to harness its energy and make it the secret behind our success.

Now, let's look at the human impact of disruption – and in particular, the degree to which it creates comfort or discomfort.

Beyond comfort

The concept of a comfort zone is familiar to most of us. Within the context of disruption and the conundrums it creates, our comfort zone comes down to one thing: what we believe we know.

Or, to put it slightly differently, the extent to which we *think* we know the answers to known questions.

When confronted by a conundrum, the more we believe we *know* the answers to the following kinds of questions, the further inside our comfort zone we feel.

- What has happened?
- Why did it happen?
- What does it mean?
- What should I do about it?
- How do I make that happen?
- What do I do next?

But what is our comfort zone and why does it matter?

The creatures of comfort

Our comfort zone isn't one thing. It is the fusion of five things, and I call them our five creatures of comfort. They are: Certainty, Clarity, Congruence, Control and Contentment.

Figure 8 - The creatures of comfort make our comfort zone warm and inviting

Certainty   Clarity   Congruence   Control   Contentment

- *Certainty* makes us feel like we know the answers we need for a specific situation. It makes us feel confident and prepared to give something a go. It also helps us to feel independent, because we have what we need to do what needs to be done.

- *Clarity* enables us to understand and make sense of what's going on. When this creature of comfort is around, we know where we are and where we are going. Clarity clears the 'fog' and helps us to see what lies ahead.

- *Congruence* is about things making sense. It involves fitting the pieces of a situation together to create an order or logic to what is happening. It's a bit like a puzzle. When we gather all the pieces and put them together, do they create the picture we expect?

- *Control* is perhaps the most powerful creature of all. It allows us to feel calm and in charge of our own destiny. Control gives us the space we need to think, and the power to make considered choices.

- *Contentment* is the 'Zen-like' creature of comfort. It makes us feel positive and generally good about what's going on. Contentment leaves us feeling safe, warm and kind of cosy.

On the Wheel of Disruption, the further our responses move towards the centre, the more certain we tend to be and the more we feel like we know what we're doing. Inside our comfort zone, we have a greater level of clarity, our future seems clearer and there is congruence because the situation makes sense. When we feel we're in control, we feel like we're in charge, and contentment means we feel relaxed and unpressured.

Figure 9 - How disruption impacts our comfort zone

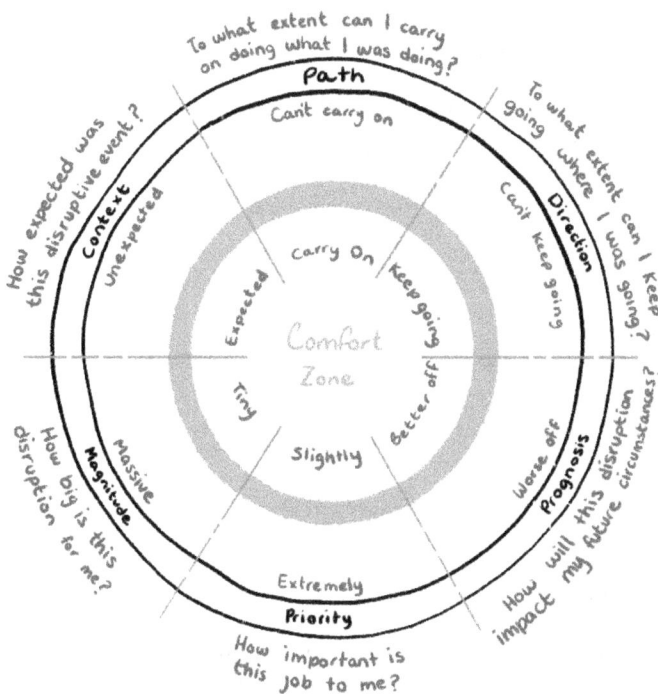

Now let's look at this within the context of getting from [A] to [B].

Cruising in our comfort zone

If we're at the centre of the Wheel of Disruption, then our journey from [A] to [B] will be straightforward and pretty much, friction-free. There are no obstacles to be navigated because we know the answers to any questions we might have.

Our team's ability to cruise along in the comfort zone has its advantages. For example, team members feel unpressured and have time to think. Ironically, however, when we're inside our comfort zone, we often don't need time to think because we already know what we need to know. This means we can pretty much switch to autopilot.

Figure 10 - When cruising in our comfort zone, we can put our brains in autopilot

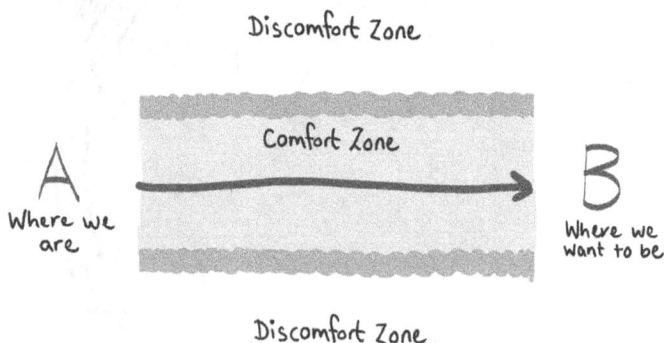

Discomfort Zone

Comfort Zone

A
Where we
are

B
Where we
want to be

Discomfort Zone

Crinkly Conundrums

But what if the disruption turns out to be more of a tremor, rather than a rumble? Even if it is, because we have a lot of experience, we still feel we *know* most of the answers to the questions that arise. On the Wheel of Disruption, these conundrums have most of our responses falling around about the middle and we feel mostly within our comfort zone.

For example, take the conundrum that I introduced a few chapters ago.

I was **driving to work**	BUT	my usual route was blocked off	SO	I ended up being 15 minutes late

This is a *Crinkly Conundrum* and it's the type that life throws at us quite regularly.

A Crinkly Conundrum makes our path look like a crinkly potato chip viewed from the side. Instead of being able to surge full speed ahead, disruption creates an obstacle. To move forward, we need to either go around it, or slow down and go over it. It's a bit like coming across a speed bump on the road.

Crinkly Conundrums are inconvenient and might be frustrating, but they don't completely stop us in our tracks. Most importantly, Crinkly Conundrums don't take us outside our comfort zone.

In the above example, I had lived in the same area for 15 years. I had been going to the same workplace for 5 years and had experienced this same disruption multiple times before. It was still inconvenient, and therefore a few of my creatures of comfort were thrown off balance. However, overall, they were more comfortable than not.

If I were to draw this conundrum in terms of [A] to [B], it would look something like the following.

Figure 11 - Crinkly Conundrums are inconvenient but familiar. They are the ones we encounter every day.

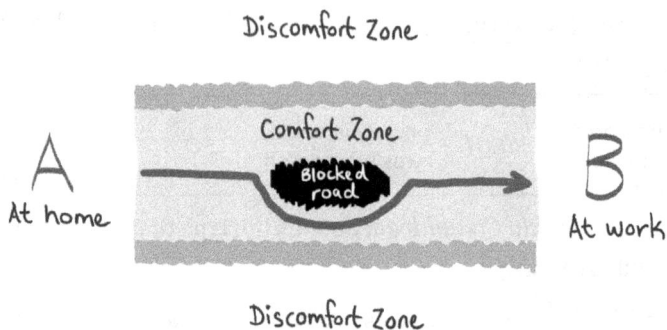

The job was getting from home to work and the disruption interfered with my standard path. I did have to think for a moment, but I didn't need to learn anything new because I already knew my options.

The journey would look less straightforward and more 'crinkly' than the first example, but I would remain inside my comfort zone.

Curly Conundrums

So what happens when an event creates a seismic shift in our situation, and takes us towards the outer rim of the Wheel of Disruption?

Consider the parrot's appearance in the pipe.

The team attended what they initially believed to be a straightforward job. However, the appearance of the parrot changed all of that. It was completely unexpected and was located in the middle of the path they needed to follow to fix the pipe. The team couldn't continue in the same direction, because they now had the life of the parrot to consider.

None of the team members wanted to kill the parrot. Therefore, when the second disruption occurred and the slippery pipe required a high-pressure hose, the situation became even more complex.

As a result, the maintenance team found themselves caught in a *Curly Conundrum*. This refers to a multi-layered situation in which multiple, interdependent events become entangled.

Even though the team was highly experienced, when the parrot turned up, they could no longer proceed with 'business as usual' to unblock the pipe. The discovery of the parrot created gaps in what had previously been a well-trodden, well-known path.

Figure 12 - Curly Conundrums make the path more 'curly' and push it into our discomfort zone

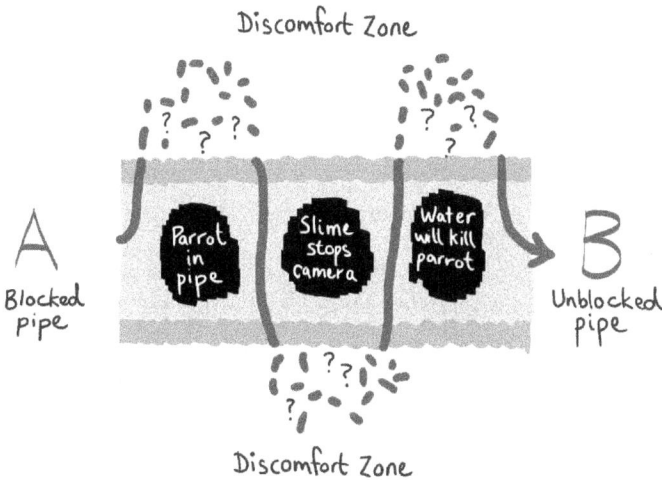

In order to close these knowledge gaps and re-build the path from [A] to [B], James Mitchell and his team needed to *know* more. To do this, they needed to venture outside their comfort zone and create a new path. This meant asking *new questions* and finding *new answers*.

Questions like:

- How do you remove a parrot from a sewer pipe?
- Are there other ways to clean slime off a pipe without using a high-pressure hose?
- What possibilities might we have overlooked?

The only way to address this conundrum and complete the job, was for James and his team to turn off autopilot and think very differently.

The critters of chaos

Have you ever seen the Steven Spielberg movie "Gremlins"? Back in the 1980s, this film introduced us to the cute, large-eyed furry creatures called the *Mogwai*. However, they came with a warning.

Never, ever, feed them after midnight. Otherwise, the adorable *Mogwai* would transform into vicious, reptilian creatures of horror called *Gremlins*.

Our creatures of comfort are like the *Mogwai*. They leave us feeling good.

Curly Conundrums create gaps in our knowledge which in turn create gaps in the path from where we *are* to where we *need* to be. When this happens, we need to venture beyond our comfort zone. However, like feeding the *Mogwai* after midnight, when our creatures of comfort cross with us into our discomfort zone, they transform into something less friendly and significantly less helpful. Namely, the critters of chaos.

When this happens: Certainty becomes Uncertainty, Clarity gives way to Confusion, Congruence becomes Clutter, Control transitions to Helplessness, and Contentment turns into Concern.

Figure 13 - The critters of chaos

Uncertainty Confusion Clutter Helplessness Concern

- *Uncertainty* makes us feel like anything could happen at any time. We feel on edge and less prepared to step forward, in case something unexpected happens. Uncertainty can also create an urge to hold on to what we know, even if it's wrong or no longer relevant.

- *Confusion* is like a tornado with bits and pieces of the situation flying around inside our heads. When we're confused, it can be hard to find a starting point and consequently, we end up just standing still.

- *Clutter* creates a sense of having many different pieces, but none of them fit together. When there is clutter, it's hard to work out how different parts relate to each other. This, in turn, makes it more difficult to determine what's important and what isn't.

- *Helplessness* leaves us feeling powerless and at the mercy of what is going on. It can lead to us giving up or giving in, due to the belief that nothing we do will make a difference anyway.

- *Concern* leads to worry and eventually fear. It makes us feel unsafe and therefore less willing to try new things, explore the unknown and take risks.

On the Wheel of Disruption, the more we find ourselves moving towards the outer rim, the more intense the five critters of chaos become.

The Discomfort Dilemma

When the critters of chaos show up, our brain instinctively reacts. It gets ready to fight, flee or freeze. It releases chemicals into our body that build up the energy to act and reinstate our beloved creatures of comfort.

It's in that moment that we experience the *Discomfort Dilemma*. I think of it as being similar to one of those never-ending staircase sketches by the artist, Escher. You know the ones: line drawings that at first glance look like the staircase is going up, but if you follow it with your finger, you end up going around in circles.

When we're facing a Curly Conundrum, we need to acquire knowledge in order to develop a new way to get the disrupted job done. To do this, we need to venture into our discomfort zone.

Once we are there, we need to learn, ask questions, develop answers, create insights and make decisions. These processes enable us to find alternative options and put the path from [A] to [B] back together again, so we can continue on our way.

Then, the critters of chaos show up. At the exact moment we need our brain to give us the time and space to rethink and respond to our Curly Conundrum, our survival instincts drive us to react and retreat.

That's when we get stuck in the Discomfort Dilemma. We can't go back to the previous path because it now has gaps in it. And, we can't go forward either, because we need new knowledge, but our brain won't let us do the thinking that's needed to develop the necessary insights.

When our team is caught in the Discomfort Dilemma, the effects become amplified. Every individual experiences the disruption differently, and this aggravates the critters of chaos even more.

Figure 14 - Our critters of chaos lead us into the Discomfort Dilemma

The big question, of course, is how do we overcome it?

Or even better, how do we take the energy that the Discomfort Dilemma creates and turn it into something that propels us forward, instead of pulling us backward?

That's where Curly Conversations come in and that's where we'll go in Part 2.

HOW SHOULD WE RESPOND to the un-
HOW DO WE BUILD TRUST? EXPECTED?
HOW DO WE HOW DO WE THINK DIFFERENTLY
ENGAGE ARE WE KEEPING HOW DO WE GET ON THE
OUR PEOPLE HOW DO OUR PROMISES? SAME PAGE?
COULD WE CHALLENGE OLD HABITS?
WE MAKE HOW DO WE CONNECT BETTER
BETTER WITH EACH OTHER? TO INTEGRITY?
CHOICES WHAT DOES IT MEAN WITH
DO WE FILL DO WE LEARN FROM OUR MISTAKES?
WHAT WE HAVE YOUR STRATEGY DOING ITS JOB?
DO WE HAVE MEANINGFUL HOW DO WE HARNESS THE POWER
PRIORITIES? ARE WE DISCIPLINED OF PURPOSE
DO WE TAKE DO WE SEIZE ENOUGH?
THE RIGHT OUR OPPORTUNITIES
RISKS?

Part 2:

THE
CONVERSATION
CONTINUUM

Curly, not chaotic

Aconversation is an indispensable tool for any team caught in a Curly Conundrum. Just imagine what would have happened in the parrot scenario if James and his team had been unable to talk through their unexpected situation.

However, some conversations are more useful than others.

Chaotic Conversations

The course of a river is shaped by the mountains and the valleys that surround it.

The Discomfort Dilemma causes the natural flow of conversations to become chaotic. Like a river spreading over the rubble of a recent earthquake, team members find themselves trying to progress from [A] to [B], with no path to follow.

Consequently, the conversations become *chaotic*.

For the team members involved, this feels like the discussion is 'all over the place' with little progress being made. This has them craving their creatures of comfort more than ever and wishing they could stick with the status quo.

Frustrated, confused and exhausted

Chaotic Conversations have people leaving the room feeling frustrated, more confused, and mentally and emotionally exhausted. These conversations also waste precious time that could be more productively spent elsewhere.

Chaotic Conversations do little to confront the conundrum that is preventing our team from doing its job. Instead, they cause the issue to splinter, creating greater complexity, and fragmenting our team's attention, efforts and relationships.

Consequently, our team spends a lot of energy and resources without achieving the desired outcome.

Caving in to compromise

If [A] is where we are and [B] is where we want to be, Chaotic Conversations often lead us to a new point – [C]. That is the *Compromised goal*. This is the one we eventually accept, because we're so exhausted and 'over it' that we just want to get on with doing something else.

So, if the Discomfort Dilemma makes conversations chaotic, even though they are the best tool for our teams to confront curly conundrums, what are we to do?

As you may have guessed, that's where Curly Conversations come in.

Curly Conversations

A Curly Conversation is a structured interaction that enables two or more people to collectively, calmly and confidently navigate a Curly Conundrum.

Curly Conversations happen by design, not default. They enable groups of people to think things through before taking action. As such, Curly Conversations are the critical precursor for collaboration.

Focused, confident and energised

Unlike its chaotic counterpart, when a team has a Curly Conversation, team members leave the room feeling focused, confident and energised. The time, effort and expense invested in bringing people together (physically or virtually) leads to stronger connections and creates significant value. This means that afterwards, when team members take action, it is both purposeful and aligned.

A Curly Conversation also helps to crystallise the issue, so it is clear to everyone in the team where they are starting from, what needs to be done and how to make it happen. This supports collaboration, builds trust and avoids potentially painful and costly errors further down the track.

Different conversations drive different levels of team performance

	Chaotic Conversations	Curly Conversations
People	Frustrated Confused Exhausted	Focused Confident Energised
Productivity	High cost Pointless action Cause future errors	High value Purposeful action Avoid future errors
Progress	Splinter the issue Go everywhere Cause inertia Job doesn't get done	Crystallise the issue Go forward Build momentum Job gets done
Performance	Underwhelming	Unbeatable

Three strands of success

Curly Conversations are deliberately designed to address Curly Conundrums. They are held together by three strands of success:

- Calm the critters
- Create connections
- Build cognitive confidence

Calm the critters

Energy drives engagement, but only when the balance is right.

This strand is underpinned by something that psychologists have known for over a century. It's often referred to as the Yerkes-Dodson Law (named after early 20th Century psychologists Robert Yerkes and John Dodson)[2].

They were among the first researchers to show that performance is directly affected by the level of psychological energy a person has. Too little or too much energy results in poorer performance.

When we're caught in a Curly Conundrum, the conversation we have in our team needs the right balance of energy. If people are too comfortable, then the conversation becomes boring or people become complacent. On the other hand, if the critters of chaos are allowed to run rampant, we run into the Discomfort Dilemma, and our team members experience too much energy. This leads to a Chaotic Conversation.

Curly Conversations however, calm the critters of chaos, by rechannelling the energy that accompanies discomfort into something that is positive and engaging.

There are many ways to do this.

For example, we can bring what is known and what is unknown into the same conversation. This creates more of a balance and means that our team members feel less 'stranded' in the unknown.

Another way is to focus on one curl at a time.

When the job we're doing is straightforward, it makes sense to see the journey from [A] to [B] as a single, continuous path. However, when our team experiences a Curly Conundrum, seeing all the way from [A] to [B] is rarely possible.

If we look back at the parrot in the pipe conundrum, there were three curls. That is, three places where the path went into the unknown and therefore had to be rebuilt.

Figure 15 - The parrot in the pipe was a three curl conversation

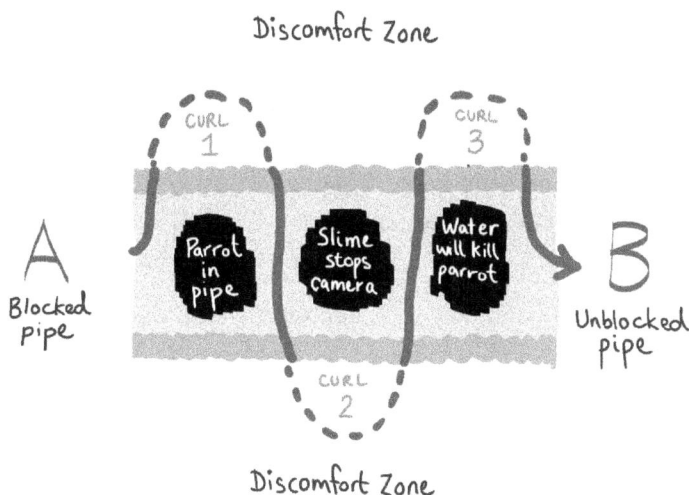

Discomfort Zone

CURL 1

CURL 3

A
Blocked pipe

Parrot in pipe

Slime stops camera

Water will kill parrot

B
Unblocked pipe

CURL 2

Discomfort Zone

A curl-by-curl approach enables our team to constantly learn and adapt as new information comes to light. It also means that the conundrums are less overwhelming and therefore, more comfortable for everyone to work through together.

Create connections

Curly Conundrums require the right connections to be made. Unfortunately, in the discomfort zone, connections are easily broken.

That's why Curly Conversations connect heads, hearts and hands.

These conversations are designed to make sense of confusing and unpredictable situations. In our heads, they help us to connect the dots and construct a coherent version of what is going on.

Connecting hearts is about ensuring that conversations are about the things that matter. Curly Conundrums require teams to put in extra effort. Why would anyone want to do that unless the topic was something they cared about?

Connecting hands involves making sure that the work is driven by a clear outcome that everyone understands. It also means that when team members get into the work, they don't lose their way in the detail and continue to head in the right direction.

Ultimately, Curly Conversations are about providing the structure, environment and opportunity for team members to connect as humans, not just problem-solving machines. Nurturing this human connection makes these conversations feel light, refreshing and enjoyable. They also build a sense of cohesion. This feeling of "we're all in this together" lasts well beyond the initial conversations and means that important jobs get done.

Build cognitive confidence

Addressing a Curly Conundrum requires us to use our brains in a way that's different to the way it is used for more routine challenges. For instance, think about the questions that the maintenance team needed to answer when they found the parrot.

When we try to think beyond what we know, and we don't know where to start, it can feel kind of 'clunky'.

To illustrate what I mean, I'd like you to do a quick exercise.

Think back to the last time you brushed your teeth. Mentally walk your way through the process for around ten seconds.

✄

Okay. Having done that, how easy would you say it was?

I am guessing that it was probably pretty easy. Right?

But let's try something different.

I'd like you to imagine brushing your teeth again. This time, however, I want you to imagine doing it using your elbows instead of your hands.

- *Did you notice how your thinking just changed?*
- *Did you feel that 'clunk' in your head, as your brain when, "Huh?"*

This *cognitive clunkiness* can tempt us to stay with our current way of thinking. It's just easier.

However, when we have *cognitive confidence* we are able to trust our brains to think in different ways when we need them to. This takes time, the right structure and most of all, practice.

That's why Curly Conversations are designed to help team members make the cognitive shift from clunkiness to confidence. The ability to make this shift enables team members to engage more easily with new ideas and think collectively, not merely as individuals. Also, the one-curl-at-a-time approach mentioned earlier, means that Curly Conversations tend to be shorter and more frequent. This provides the opportunity for regular practice.

You'll be able to experience this first-hand in Part 4, when you use the Curly Conversation Starters with your team.

✁

When we pull the three strands above together, what will Curly Conversations give you and your team?

Figure 16 - The three strands of success

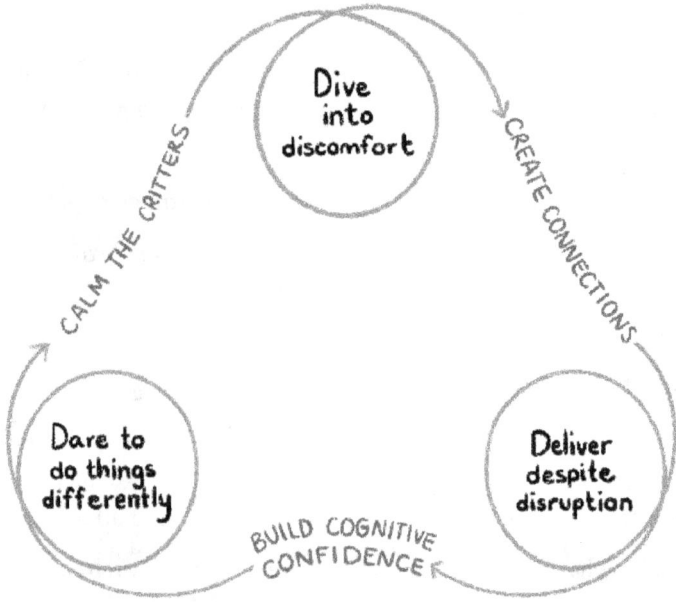

By calming the critters of chaos and creating the right connections, your team will be energised and willing to dive into discomfort together.

Similarly, with more time to think and greater cognitive confidence, your team will dare to do things differently.

When all these elements come together, Curly Conversations will enable your team to confront its curliest conundrums and ultimately, deliver results despite disruption.

Time to reflect

Let's pause for a moment here and come back to the example from your own team.

We've already talked about what kind of conundrum you were facing and whether it put your team inside or outside its comfort zone. So now we can think about the following:

- *Were there signs of the Discomfort Dilemma in your team?*
- *What did they look like?*
- *What kind of conversation did you have?*

Now think more broadly.

- *When you consider your team's way of working, would you say that its conversations tend to be more Chaotic or Curly?*
- *How would you rate them out of ten?*

1	2	3	4	5	6	7	8	9	10

⟵——————————————————————⟶

When we're in our discomfort zone, our team's conversations are always **chaotic**

When we're in our discomfort zone, our team's conversations are always **curly**

The more disrupted our environment, the more time our team will spend in its discomfort zone. So, if in the assessment above, your team was more towards 1 and you'd like it to be more towards 10, how do you make that happen?

The answer is coming up next.

Curly capability roadmap

When an accomplished chef creates a magnificent meal, it's not an accident. It's the result of the chef's ability to bring many elements together in just the right way. For instance, the right ingredients, the right oven temperature, the right preparation techniques and so on.

Of course, no one wakes up one day and suddenly discovers that they are a master chef. It takes time.

If you or I wanted to become a chef, we might first learn to cook using a recipe. Then, as our confidence grew, we'd probably start to modify our favourite recipes, producing *our own* version of the dish by adding a bit of personal flare.

Eventually, we'd reach the point where we could confidently create our own recipes.

But what does culinary expertise have to do with Curly Conversations?

These days, most of the Curly Conversations I lead involve hundreds of people. One of the comments that participants consistently make, is how effortless and energising these conversations feel. As one CEO described it, "It's like we have all these parts and initially we're not sure where we are going. But then, somehow, it all comes together and when we reach the end, we're amazed at how far we've come."

Like a magnificent meal, Curly Conversations don't happen by accident. They require many different elements to be purposefully brought together in just the right way and at the right time.

For example, we need to set the right outcome, ask the right questions, have the right people in the room, pick the right pace and so forth. We also need to be able to adapt questions in real time and adjust to different people's perspectives.

These and many other elements keep teams connected, deactivate the Discomfort Dilemma, and enable the team to move its collective thinking forward.

When it comes to developing your team's Curly Conversational capability, there are three stages of development.

Figure 17 - The curly capability roadmap

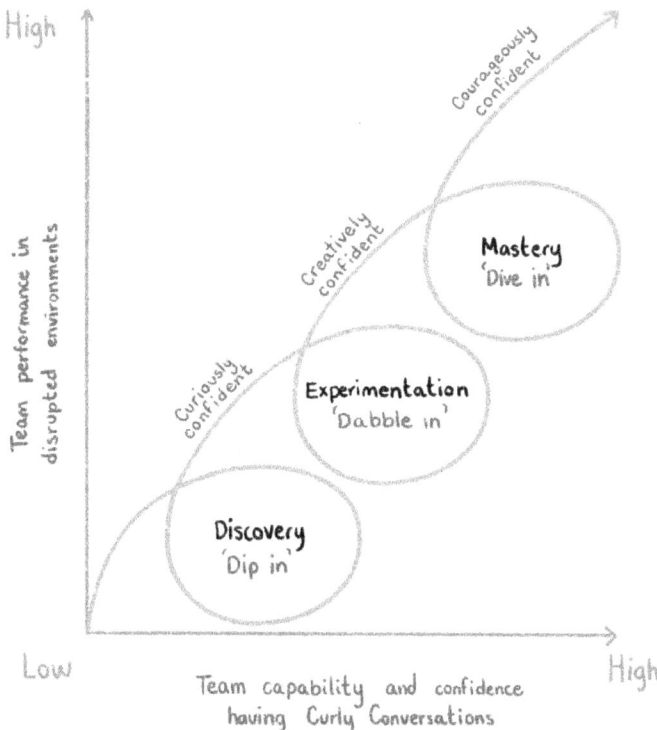

The Discovery Stage

Like a budding chef, during this first stage teams develop foundational knowledge and become familiar with what Curly Conversations feel like. They are able to do this by using the conversational equivalent of a recipe.

I call this *a conversation starter.*

The theme for this stage is immersion. Its goal is to give your team an opportunity to metaphorically dip their toe into their discomfort zone and become conscious of their response. It's also about being willing to engage in conversations that have a lot more questions than answers.

The key outcome for the Discovery Stage is to have a team that is *curiously confident.* In other words, team members are willing to dip into the discomfort of not knowing the answer, without leaping to a solution. This leaves space to open up the conversation to discovery, possibilities and insights.

In this way, this first stage is not about what we know. It's about what we don't know and whether we can confidently admit it and sit with it.

The Experimentation Stage

In this stage, teams build on their foundational knowledge and start adapting their conversational recipes to suit their own unique conundrums.

The theme for this phase is evolution. Its goal is to give teams a chance to hone the technical elements of Curly Conversations. For example, how do you ask the right question in the right way at the right time? In this way, teams can start with the comfort of a recipe that works, and then evolve it to make it their own.

A key outcome for the Experimentation Stage is to have a team that is *creatively confident*. It brings in a playful element and a willingness to dabble in discomfort and try new things that may or may not work.

The Experimentation Stage is also about team members learning to consciously switch their mindset from autopilot, everyday thinking to manual, or curly thinking.

When a team is both creatively confident and team members can switch from autopilot to curly thinking, they are free to do things differently and able to let go of the status quo.

The Mastery Stage

The Mastery Stage's theme is growth. Unlike the other stages, this stage of conversational development involves teams enhancing their Curly Conversations along not one, but four dimensions.

The first dimension is *design*. During this stage, teams go beyond understanding *how* Curly Conversations work, and learn *why* they work that way. This gives flexibility and allows your team members to design their own conversations and create their own conversational recipes.

The second dimension is *efficiency*. This involves making the shift from pre-prepared conversations to being able to design conversations in real time.

The third dimension is *complexity*. During the Mastery Stage, your team becomes adept at navigating increasingly disrupted and complex situations.

Finally, there is the fourth dimension: *scale*. When team members pursue conversational mastery, they develop their ability to have more Curly Conversations with other teams and with more people. When starting out, the focus is on having Curly Conversations one-to-one or within one team. However, with time and experience, this capability can be expanded to multiple conversations with multiple teams across organisations. It's at this latter point that Curly Conversations become part of your organisation's DNA.

A key outcome for the Mastery Stage is to have a team that is *courageously confident*. That is, team members understand Curly Conversations so well, and feel so confident having them, that they are willing to confront curlier and more complex conundrums together. Consequently, they become willing to dive into discomfort whenever it's required.

✂

So, now that we have a sense of the 'big picture' and the stages that will get us there, let's come back to you and your team. Most importantly, let's walk through the easiest way for you and your team to start having more curly and less chaotic conversations.

HOW SHOULD WE RESPOND TO THE UNEXPECTED?
HOW DO WE BUILD TRUST?
HOW DO WE HOW DO WE THINK DIFFERENTLY?
HOW DO WE ARE WE KEEPING HOW DO WE GET ON THE
ENGAGE OUR PROMISES? SAME PAGE?
OUR PEOPLE WE CHALLENGE OLD HABITS?
COULD HOW DO WE CONNECT BETTER
WE MAKE WITH EACH OTHER? TO INTEGRITY?
BETTER WHAT DOES IT MEAN HAVE
CHOICES DO WE LEARN FROM OUR MISTAKES?
DO WE HAVE IS OUR STRATEGY DOING ITS JOB?
WHAT ARE THE HOW DO WE HARNESS THE POWER
DO WE THE RIGHT SELF-DISCIPLINED OF PURPOSE
PRIORITIES. DO WE SEIZE ENOUGH?
DO WE TAKE OUR OPPORTUNITIES?
THE RIGHT RISKS?

PART 3:

DIP IN
AND
DISCOVER

About the toolkit

The best way to appreciate the value of a Curly Conversation is to have one. The easiest way for you and your team to do this is to use a Curly Conversation Starter. It's like a conversation recipe that provides carefully designed questions, which will guide your team through a specific Curly Conundrum.

The last part of this book includes 15 conversation starters about common team challenges. Each synthesises lessons from thousands of Curly Conversations I've led across the world.

These Curly Conversation Starters will enable you and your team to gently dip into discomfort and get a feel for the difference that a Curly Conversation can make.

But before we go to Part 4, let's address what Curly Conversation Starters are and how they will help you.

Create the space

Curly Conversation Starters will make it easier for you and your team to create the time and space these important conversations need. They do so by breaking conversations into bite-sized chunks that can be covered in 50 minutes.

Also, because they are shorter and easier to schedule, you and your team can have Curly Conversations when you need them, not just when you can find half a day in your diary. This also means that you can have Curly Conversations more often, making them more familiar and effective through practice.

Build trust

Curly Conversation Starters will make it easier for everyone in the team to say what they think, even on controversial issues.

When I ask people why their conversations are chaotic, one of the most common reasons they give me is that they feel their environment, or their meetings, are not psychologically safe.

People feeling unsafe is often a consequence of a disrupted environment where Chaotic Conversations are the norm. Chaotic conversations often mean that important jobs fail to get completed. However, due to the chaos, it can be difficult to identify the reason for the failure.

One of the first things we ask when something goes wrong is "*Why* did this happen?" But when we are unable to identify what caused something to go wrong, we still want an answer. So, we change the question, often unconsciously, to "*Who* made this happen?"

A team or business that is dominated by Chaotic Conversations is frequently accompanied by a history of blaming, rather than learning from mistakes. This invariably causes people to be reluctant to take risks and say what is really on their mind.

So, how will *Curly Conversation Starters* help?

These *Curly Conversation Starters* are designed to enable your team to have better conversations when it's in its discomfort zone. This book asks the questions that need to be answered, without any political agenda or bias. This objectivity and the fact that no one in the room needs to ask the important (yet, sometimes difficult) questions, helps unlock the door to otherwise challenging topics.

Also, having Curly Conversations regularly makes difficult topics more and more familiar. Therefore, they become increasingly easy to raise and talk about. Also, the design of *Curly Conversation Starters* will enable your team to warm up by talking about the less scary, 'baby elephants' in the room, before attempting to tackle their bigger counterparts.

Make thinking easier

The *Curly Conversation Starters* have been designed to make it easier for team members to switch their brains from autopilot to manual.

Each conversation starter begins with a simple, engaging story that links to the topic being discussed. This has been designed to activate different thinking muscles and trigger the more curious mindset that a Curly Conversation needs.

It means that you can schedule your meeting in the middle of a busy day and still have a thought-provoking conversation.

Turn energy into engagement

Curly Conversation Starters will help you and your team to generate the energy needed to have a different kind of conversation.

Each conversation starter is based on a simple, yet effective principle.

Find a challenge that people are collectively motivated to address, and the energy and momentum will follow.

For example, imagine that a loved one called you to say that they were locked out of their house and their car keys were inside.

This meant that they were unable to pick up their two and three-year-old from the childcare centre.

- *How energised and motivated would your loved one be to find a solution?*

- *How motivated and energised would you be to find a way to help them and ensure their kids weren't stranded?*

Now, what would happen if the same scenario involved a complete stranger or someone you didn't like?

- *Would you be equally motivated to engage in the conversation?*

The key to engagement lies in the 'care factor', i.e., how much your team members care about something. These conversation starters give your team members the opportunity to choose the topics that *they* care about. This makes it easier for everyone to engage and be part of the conversation from the very beginning.

Design the right questions

Finally, *Curly Conversation Starters* take the preparation time and pressure out of designing the right questions.

The questions in each conversation ensure there is a beginning, a middle and an end. This means that team members can focus on sharing, listening and learning, rather than worrying about what question to ask next.

✂

When incorporated into your team's regular rhythm, *Curly Conversation Starters* provide a simple way to improve your team's conversational capability. They will also have your team feeling more connected, more confident and more energised when confronting its curliest conundrums.

All of these will support greater collaboration, better business outcomes and improved team performance.

What to do now

Now that we've talked about Curly Conversations, what they are and why we need them, we can get on with actually *having* one. But what do you need to do to set up your conversations to succeed?

As I mentioned earlier, Part 4 contains 15 conversation starters.

Each 50-minute conversation follows the same format. Once you've had a few conversations, your team will find its own rhythm. To start with, I'd suggest the following:

1. **READ** the short 'thought prompter' – 5 minutes

2. **REFLECT** – Reflect on these questions in pairs – 5 minutes

3. **RESPOND** – Explore the answers to these questions as a full team – 30 minutes

4. **REVIEW** – Discuss these questions and collaboratively agree where you'd like to go next – 10 minutes

The five conversation categories

The Curly Conversation Starters have been divided into five categories. Together these provide the essential foundation from which any team can deliver its strategy and create value.

The categories are:

- **Connect better** – build a sense of trust and cohesion as a team
- **Be better** – learn together and continuously improve
- **Work Smarter** – achieve better outcomes more effectively
- **Make better choices** – focus on the things that matter
- **Embrace change** – capture the opportunity of disruption

Start by simply sitting down with your team, choose which conversations are most relevant. Then, work through one of these conversations each time you meet.

Practical tips for success

Let this book be your tour guide

✓ Each team member will need their own copy of *Curly Conversations for Teams* so they can write their reflections in it as they go along. Also, because you'll be asking the team to have a different kind of conversation, reading this book first ensures that everyone starts with a shared understanding and mindset.

✓ When someone new joins the team, make *Curly Conversations for Teams* part of their induction program.

✓ When having the Curly Conversation, remove everything, except this book, from the table. This book acts as a signal that the team is about to have a different kind of conversation.

Schedule conversations in advance

✓ Ideally, schedule Curly Conversations around 2 or 3 weeks apart. Remember, this is about creating a rhythm and familiarity.

✓ If you intend to include the Curly Conversations in a regular team meeting, make it the first item on your agenda. This will set a positive tone for all the other conversations that follow.

Resist the river

✓ There will be times, especially if your environment or team have been disrupted, when you will feel a sense of urgency and a desire to seek crisp answers. Consequently, you will be tempted to react to the chaos, instead of pausing and asking questions. It is in these moments that Chaotic Conversations are born.

✓ The good news is that you and your team will be better positioned to consciously choose whether you want that to happen.

Use the questions

✓ The questions in each Curly Conversation Starter have been designed in a particular way. Follow the sequence.

✓ Some conversations may need more time. If your team is really engaged and you're having a rich conversation, but you've only reached the fourth question, don't worry. You're having a Curly Conversation that needs to be had. Instead of rushing through the remaining questions, consider continuing the same topic next time.

If you do this, when you bring the current conversation to a close, ensure that someone in the team is responsible for doing a short summary of the conversation so far. Also, encourage team members to note down their thoughts in their book. Doing both of these will make it easier to pick up the conversation next time.

If you're uncomfortable, you're on the right track

✓ When we've been running at speed and suddenly find ourselves with some space to think, it can feel a little strange. Some of my clients say that they feel a bit 'antsy' or 'jittery'. Most of our lives we're taught to speed towards results and tick off achievements. Curly Conversations require a more considered and purposeful pace.

So, if you or members of your team feel this way, relax. It means that what you're doing is working.

Reach out for a conversation

The ability to have Curly Conversations is a critical capability for any team that is operating within a disrupted environment. This book provides an easy and practical way for you to get your team started.

To take this capability to the next level or for more tools, guidance or support programs visit **www.curlyconversations.com**

How should we respond to the un-expected? How do we build trust? How do we think differently? How do we engage our people? Are we keeping our promises? How do we get on the same page? We challenge old habits? How could we make better choices? How do we connect better with each other? Do we lead with integrity? What does it mean... Do we learn from our mistakes? Is our strategy doing its job? How do we harness the power? Do we have the right priorities? Do we take the right risks? Are we disciplined & purpose? Do we seize enough of our opportunities?

PART 4:

CURLY CONVERSATION STARTERS

Connect better

Build trust

Leaps of greatness require the combined problem-solving ability of people who trust each other.

Simon Sinek

Have you ever considered the difference between a conversation and a chat?

The word 'conversation' comes from the Latin term *conversari*, meaning 'to live among'. It later evolved in middle English into *converse*, meaning to 'live among and be familiar with'. These days, conversation is used to refer to "a talk between two or more people in which thoughts, feelings, and ideas are expressed, questions are asked and answered, or news and information is exchanged"[3].

A *chat,* however, only takes into account the first half of this definition. It refers to "talking in an informal or friendly way"[4].

In my experience, great conversations have four characteristics: they engage their participants, invite considered and open contribution and bring people closer together. In addition to this, great conversations trigger positive change.

All these characteristics have a common element threading through them:

Trust.

Without trust, people cling to the certainty of the status quo and resist entering the unknown. They also step back and create distance when the conversation needs them to step forward. Lack of trust also affects the openness of contributions and makes people less likely to listen and say what they think. And finally, when trust is absent, it drives a wedge between people, causing them to become disconnected.

Great conversations help to build trust. However, in order to have great conversations, there needs to be a level of trust to start with. This symbiotic relationship sometimes causes us to become tied up in knots.

There is also another challenge.

Have you ever noticed how, when someone in a team mentions trust, the tension can actually increase?

It can mean that our intentions backfire and instead of building trust, it feels like we lose it?

But how can we have great conversations if we need trust, but can't talk about it?

I'm a pragmatist, which means that I view the concept of trust through a very practical lens. I've also spent many years leading Curly Conversations in some pretty intense, high-stakes situations.

Trust doesn't happen because we talk about it. Trust happens when we forget about it completely. Instead of talking about it and how much of it we have or don't have, we focus on learning something, achieving something or building something amazing together. When we do this, trust becomes a natural consequence, not an obstacle.

Trust is a team sport. As soon as we see ourselves as players in the game, not commentators, we create the conditions for trust to emerge on its own.

Curly questions to consider

Reflect in pairs

What is trust?

_____

_____

_____

_____

What role do I play in building trust within a team?

_____

_____

_____

_____

Respond as a team

How is this article relevant for us?

_____

_____

_____

_____

What's the biggest challenge we face at the moment, as a team?

_____

_____

_____

_____

What would happen if each of us approached this challenge from a position of 100 percent trust?

_____

_____

_____

_____

How would it influence our conversations?

_____

_____

_____

_____

How would it impact our performance?

_____

_____

_____

_____

Review and look forward

What one thing could we change to make this a reality?

_____

_____

_____

_____

Is it worth doing?

_____

_____

_____

_____

How do we make it happen?

_____

_____

_____

_____

Create alignment

There are always two people in every picture: The photographer and the viewer.

Ansel Adams

In any situation, our perspective influences our response. I was reminded of this recently when a friend told me the following story:

It was just before lunch at the local primary school and it was reading time. The teacher gave the instructions, "Go and grab your reading books everyone and find a partner. Then, sit down quietly and take turns reading to each other from your books."

Five minutes later, most of the children were sitting down with their reading partners, except for one boy. He was standing in the middle of the room yelling at the top of his voice.

The teacher marched over to the boy with an annoyed look on her face and sternly asked him why he was yelling.

"I couldn't find a reading partner," explained the boy. "I looked for one, but all the other kids were taken. I was yelling out 'I don't have a reading partner' to let others know that they could read with me if they wanted to."

The teacher frowned and asked the boy, "Do you think that standing in the middle of the classroom and yelling is the most effective way to find a partner? Can you think of a better way?"

The boy paused to reflect. "Not really," he answered. "What would be a better way?"

"Well," said the teacher, "You could go and talk quietly to each person to see if they wanted a partner."

"But that wouldn't be more effective at all," responded the boy. "I would have to go randomly to each person and interrupt them when I could see they already had a partner. So, that option would be less effective for me *and* for them," he explained.

The teacher smiled and nodded. She had to admit, she could see where the boy was coming from.

After a while she said, "Okay. This lunchtime, I want you to do something for me. I want you to come up with a better way of finding a reading partner. One that doesn't involve yelling in the classroom."

The boy went out to lunch and when the bell rang to return to class, he went up to his teacher.

"I've thought about it and I've got the perfect way," he proclaimed triumphantly. "When it is time to read, anyone who needs a partner should go and stand in that corner of the room. That way everyone will know, and the right people will be able to find each other."

It was a simple and effective solution. From then on, in that classroom and all the other classrooms across the school, that was how reading time was done.

Curly questions to consider

Reflect in pairs

Which perspective can you relate to most easily in this story? The boy's or the teacher's?

_____

_____

_____

_____

Why do you think that is?

_____

_____

_____

_____

Respond as a team

What does the word 'alignment' mean?

_____

_____

_____

_____

How does our perspective influence the way we connect with one another?

_____

_____

_____

_____

If we were aligned regarding a particular challenge, what would that look and feel like?

_____

_____

_____

_____

What is the biggest challenge that we have as a team right now?

_____

_____

_____

_____

Looking at the characteristics we just talked about, how aligned are we regarding that challenge?

_____

_____

_____

_____

In what areas are we most or least aligned on this issue?

_____

_____

_____

_____

Review and look forward

What would need to happen to achieve full alignment?

_____

_____

_____

_____

Where should we go from here?

_____

_____

_____

_____

Keep promises

I attribute my success to this.
I never gave or accepted any excuse.

Florence Nightingale

In 1995, Pepsi ran a sales campaign called the "Pepsi Stuff Promotion". Consumers who bought Pepsi products could earn points. These could then be redeemed to get Pepsi-branded merchandise.

The promotion was supported by a high-energy, television advertisement. As dramatic music blared, a hair-flicking young man was shown strutting out of his house, holding his school books. As he did so, the writing on the screen advertised what 'Pepsi stuff' the guy had acquired and how many points they had cost.

T-shirt – 75 points

Leather jacket – 1,450 points

Shades – 175 points

The scene then switched to show the cool guy's school, with windows being blown out and papers flying as hurricane-strength winds gripped the classroom. A large wheel of an aircraft landed outside the classroom and in the final scene of the advertisement, the main character was seen climbing out of a fighter jet.

On the screen were written the words "Harrier Fighter – 7,000,000 Pepsi Points".

The plane, or at least the ability to redeem one for 7 million Pepsi points was meant to be an over-the-top joke. However, as Matt Parker explains in his book *Humble PI: When math goes wrong in the real world*[5], one person took the claim very seriously.

His name was John Leonard.

Unfortunately, when the folks at Pepsi had created the campaign, they underestimated the ease with which 7 million points could be accrued. Unlike Pepsi, John Leonard did the numbers and worked out that he could acquire 7 million Pepsi points by spending $700,000. Now, while this was (and still is) a significant amount of money, it was nothing compared to the value of the $20 million Harrier Jump Jet that was shown in the commercial.

Leonard took his 7 million points to Pepsi and demanded that they honour their commitment and give him the fighter jet.

Pepsi refused, saying it was just a joke. However, John Leonard took them to court.

After considerable arguments about what made the commercial a joke and not a serious promise, Pepsi won the case and Leonard was deprived of his Jump Jet.

Now, call me cynical, but I think that somewhere deep down, John Leonard may have known that the Pepsi advertisement wasn't being serious. However, this story still offers a great example of the fine line between intentions and interpretation.

And, when it comes to making promises, how easily that line can become blurred.

I guess the moral of the story is to only ever make promises you can keep and always keep the promises that you make.

Curly questions to consider

Reflect in pairs

How would you define 'a promise'?

_____

_____

_____

_____

Have you ever experienced a mismatch between the intention and interpretation of a promise?

_____

_____

_____

_____

What impact did it have on the people involved?

_____

_____

_____

_____

Respond as a team

How important are promises within our team?

_____

_____

_____

_____

What kinds of promises do we make to each other?

_____

_____

_____

_____

What kinds of promises do we make to other stakeholders?

_____

_____

_____

_____

How good are we at keeping promises?

_____

_____

_____

_____

What stops us from keeping promises?

_____

_____

_____

_____

What impact does this have?

_____

_____

_____

_____

Review and look forward

What is one thing we could do differently as a team?

_____

_____

_____

_____

What should we do now?

_____

_____

_____

_____

Be
better

Have integrity

Integrity is doing the right thing, even when no one is looking.

C.S. Lewis

The Gouldian Finch is arguably one of Australia's most beautiful native birds. Only ten centimetres (4 inches) in length from the top of its head to the end of its tail, this finch is like a flying rainbow, with bright bluey-green, purple, orange, yellow, black and red feathers.

For around 10 years, my family kept Gouldian Finches in a huge, heated aviary in our house. Their delicate song could be heard throughout the house. As with all pets, there was a downside. In the wintertime, the seed on the ground sometimes attracted members of the local rodent community. And, when we went away, we always needed to get someone to come in and tend to the aviary.

Eventually, we decided to stop breeding the birds and over the next 18 months, we went from having 60 birds to just two. With their beaks overgrown and their gnarled old claws pointing in all directions, these two fellas were like an old married couple.

They slept on the same branch and could always be found in the same area of the aviary. Even when one of the boys was too old to fly, the other one stayed down with him at the bottom of the cage.

Eventually, the older bird died and the last one was left on his own. He was still quite healthy and rather than leaving him to spend the rest of his days on his own, we decided to give the last bird to someone who had a large aviary. At least then the finch would have some company.

On the morning we advertised the bird, we received a call from an angry woman. She skipped 'hello' and started the conversation with an aggressive monologue.

"Do you know how long these birds live for? A five-year-old bird is not going to live very long. How dare you try to con people by selling them an old bird. You should be ashamed of yourself."

It was clear that the woman had not read our advertisement. We were giving the bird away to experienced Gouldian Finch owners who would know that a five-year-old bird was old.

When the woman finally stopped to take a breath, we explained all this to her.

"Oh," she said, still quite peeved. "Well…it's still not good," and with that she hung up.

In the end, our little finch went to an aviary of a reputable breeder, so we achieved the desired outcome. However, the experience was a useful reminder that just because you're doing the right thing, doesn't mean it's going to be easy.

Curly questions to consider

Reflect in pairs

Have you ever tried to do the right thing and found it harder than expected?

_____

_____

_____

_____

How do you know if it's the right thing or not?

_____

_____

_____

_____

Respond as a team

What role does integrity play in our team?

_____

_____

_____

_____

How easy is it for people in our team to do what's right?

_____

_____

_____

_____

Why is that?

_____

_____

_____

_____

Has there been a time when we gave up on doing the right thing due to pressure from somewhere else?

_____

_____

_____

_____

If we could go back in time, would we do anything differently?

_____

_____

_____

_____

Review and look forward

What lesson could we learn from this?

_____

_____

_____

_____

Is there anything we'd like to change?

_____

_____

_____

_____

What should we do now?

_____

_____

_____

_____

Challenge old habits

The chains of habit are too light to be felt until they are too heavy to be broken.

Warren Buffet

My daughter was in her late teens when, one day, she came into the kitchen with her arms fully outstretched and ready for a hug.

There is nothing like a hug from someone you love. As our arms closed around each other, it was like being firmly wrapped in a soft, warm blanket.

It was at that moment that my daughter spoke. She said, "Do you know, Mum? You still hug me like I'm ten."

It was kind of unexpected.

"What do you mean?" I asked.

"When you hug me, you put your arms over my shoulders as though I am shorter than you. You kind of hug my head. But Mum... here's the thing! *You* are the short one now so, technically, I should be putting my arms over your shoulders. Otherwise, I'd need to crouch down every time you give me a hug."

It was something I'd never thought about until that moment.

"So, do you want me to change?" I asked.

As it turned out, my daughter didn't want me to change the way that I was giving her hugs. She said she liked them just the way they were.

The conversation got me thinking. How easy it is for behaviours, that made sense in a different time and place, to become unconscious habits. And, how hard it is to change them unless they have our full attention.

Curly questions to consider

Reflect in pairs

What habits have you recently become aware of?

_____

_____

_____

_____

If there was one habit you could lose in an instant, what would it be?

_____

_____

_____

_____

Respond as a team

What do habits look like in a team environment?

_____

_____

_____

_____

What impact do habits have on our effectiveness?

_____

_____

_____

_____

What behaviours or actions are we doing today that used to make sense in a previous environment, but no longer make sense today?

_____

_____

_____

_____

Is the world in which those behaviours began still relevant?

_____

_____

_____

_____

Is now a good time to reflect, review and reconsider some of our behaviours?

_____

_____

_____

_____

Review and look forward

If there were one team habit that we could change for the better, what would it be?

_____

_____

_____

_____

Why haven't we changed it until now?

_____

_____

_____

_____

Where would we like to take this from here?

_____

_____

_____

_____

Learn from mistakes

When things go wrong,
don't go with them.

Elvis Presley

A while ago, I thought I'd try my hand at doing a little DIY around the house.

One of the tasks was to paint a set of cupboard doors. They were in an area where there were many textures and colours. Try as I might, after looking through hundreds of colour cards, I couldn't find the eggplanty-blacky-purply colour that I wanted.

So, I had to get creative and mix my own paints to get the colour I wanted.

It took a few goes to get it right. Adding a little bit of red, then a bit more grey and more red and so on. Eventually, I created exactly the colour I wanted. I didn't know what colours were in it, but that didn't really matter at the time. I had plenty to paint the cupboards and that was all I needed.

Then, having taken all sixteen cupboard doors off their hinges, I spent the next three-days painting. Once the paint had dried and the doors had been re-hung, I stood back from them with a sense of satisfaction.

"Not bad for a beginner!"

Alas, twenty-four hours later, that feeling had well and truly disappeared.

I noticed that the paint was taking longer than expected to dry. It scratched easily and in some areas had peeled off completely. That's when I discovered my error.

I had lovingly painted my magnificent looking cupboards with the wrong kind of paint. I had used one that was water-based when the old paint was an oil-based enamel.

I knew from my early high school science class that oil and water didn't mix. However, what my science teacher had failed to mention was if you paint water-based paint over an oil-based paint, it doesn't 'stick'. Instead, it creates a separate layer and eventually peels off.

NOOOOOOOOOOOOO!

It was a painful lesson of epic proportions. Not only did I need to re-paint the cupboards with new paint, I first needed to scrape off all the other paint I'd just spent three days applying. And, I didn't know what the colour was and so, I had to once again go through the process of working it out.

If only this had been one of those lessons I could have learnt from someone else's mistake, not my own.

Curly questions to consider

Reflect in pairs

What's the biggest mistake you've made at work?

_____

_____

_____

_____

What did you learn from it?

_____

_____

_____

_____

Respond as a team

What role does learning play in our team?

_____

_____

_____

_____

What expectations do we have regarding mistakes?

_____

_____

_____

_____

Do we tend to learn from, or repeat, mistakes?

_____

_____

_____

_____

What is the relationship between mistakes and success in our team?

_____

_____

_____

_____

Do we encourage learning enough?

_____

_____

_____

_____

Review and look forward

If we wanted to encourage more learning, what would we need to change?

_____

_____

_____

_____

How could we do that?

_____

_____

_____

_____

What should we do next?

_____

_____

_____

_____

Work
smarter

Put strategy to work

Hope is not a strategy.

Vince Lombardi

S trategy is a common topic in many teams and businesses. But, have you ever wondered why we have a strategy? I mean, if a strategy had a job description, what would it say?

Eighty-percent of leaders believe their organisation is good at formulating strategy, but only 44 percent think it's good at implementation[6].

After nearly 25 years developing and implementing strategy across the world, I've learnt that every strategy needs two critical elements, and that the second element is often overlooked.

The first element is the strategy's content. Namely, what it says about what's going on, what the challenges are and what your team is going to do about it. This is what is written on presentation slides and other documents.

The second element is your strategy's effectiveness as a delivery tool. In other words, does it do its job by making delivery as easy as possible?

It doesn't matter how much effort has been invested into developing your team's strategy or what action it promotes, if the strategy itself isn't fit for purpose.

So, how do you know if your team's strategy meets this second critical success factor?

It needs to contain five critical qualities:

1. **It clearly defines value** – Your strategy describes the kind of value your team creates and how much value is being created for your customers. It also shows how achieving this will create reciprocal value for your team.

2. **It clearly describes the desired outcome.** A strategy describes your team's intention to transition from a current state to a better future state. It therefore describes the team's intention to shift from [A] to [B]. Many strategies focus on the journey (I.e., the strategic plan). However, what's even more important is that the strategy clearly describes both the starting point and the outcome. In other words, where is [A], what will reaching [B] look like, and why this is a goal worth pursuing.

3. **It builds engagement while it is being developed.** A strategy is able to do its job when the people who are going to deliver it feel that it belongs to them. This ensures that they are willing to contribute and make change happen because they believe in the outcome.

4. **The development process aligns team members' thinking.** By the time it has been completed, an effective strategy has created a shared understanding of why it's

needed, what team challenges it addresses and why the proposed action makes sense.

5. **It supports collaborative action** – People can't work together if they don't know what is expected or if they don't know who is supposed to be doing what. Your strategy is doing its job if people know this, and also, they know how to recover when the unexpected pushes plans off course.

When your team's strategy has all five of these success factors, it will have the energy it needs to achieve momentum during delivery. It will also mean that delivery can progress faster because people are more focused and able to work together.

Curly questions to consider

Reflect in pairs

If someone asked you what our team's strategy was, how easily could you explain it?

_____

_____

_____

_____

Of the five critical qualities above, which ones stood out more than the others? Why?

_____

_____

_____

_____

Respond as a team

Which elements of this conversation starter are relevant for our team?

_____

_____

_____

_____

What role does having a strategy play in our success?

_____

_____

_____

How would we rate our strategy (from 1 to 5, with 5 being the best) in terms of having the right content and heading in the right direction?

_____

_____

_____

_____

How would we rate our strategy (out of 5) in terms of meeting the *five critical qualities* described above?

_____

_____

_____

_____

How would others who are in our team, but not in this conversation, rate our strategy?

_____

_____

_____

_____

How is this rating impacting the way we deliver change?

_____

_____

_____

_____

Review and look forward

Is there an opportunity for us to improve in this area?

_____

_____

_____

_____

Where should we go from here?

_____

_____

_____

_____

Harness the power of purpose

First they ignore you, then they laugh at you, then they fight you, then you win.

Mahatma Gandhi

In 1873, Tilly Aston was born in the town of Carisbrook, Australia. Tilly was visually impaired at birth and by the time she was seven years old, she was completely blind. At the age of eight, her father died.

Tilly's future was looking pretty bleak, until she had a chance meeting with someone who changed her life forever.

Thomas James was a miner who had lost his sight in an accident at work. He taught Tilly to read braille. So began many years of formal education. Unfortunately, it came to an abrupt halt at Melbourne University. Tilly was the first blind person to enrol in an Arts degree, and consequently, there weren't enough books written in braille to enable her to complete her studies. She left in her second year, having suffered a nervous breakdown.

This was the first of many situations Tilly found herself in where she felt excluded from education because of her blindness. It fuelled a deep determination and sense of purpose in her.

Tilly started writing books in braille and became an advocate for the rights of blind people. Among her many achievements, she founded The Association for the Advancement of the Blind, which is now called Vision Australia. Her relentless lobbying achieved voting rights and led to new laws being introduced to help people who were blind to live independently. In 1913, Tilly became the head of the Victorian Education Department's School for the Blind.

Tilly Aston was powered by purpose. She refused to allow adversity to stand between her and significant social and political change. In the Kings Domain Gardens in Melbourne, there is a bell dedicated to her memory. Around the bottom edge there is a quote from one of Tilly's many books:

"Poor eyes limit your sight. Poor vision limits your deeds."

A powerful purpose and vision provide an inner drive or energy. They provide the propulsion we need to overcome the obstacles that life throws our way. Without this drive, we become distracted by the things we don't have, and therefore, we allow them to hold us back.

Curly questions to consider

Reflect in pairs

Can you think of a time when you felt you had a strong sense of purpose?

_____

_____

_____

_____

What did it feel like?

_____

_____

_____

_____

Respond as a team

What does it mean to have a sense of purpose?

_____

_____

_____

_____

Where does our sense of purpose come from?

_____

_____

_____

_____

How well defined is our team's purpose?

_____

_____

_____

_____

If a sculpture were created to represent our team's purpose, what would the sculpture be of?

_____

_____

_____

_____

What would the sculpture's title be?

_____

_____

_____

_____

Does our purpose give us the energy we need to succeed?

_____

_____

_____

_____

Review and look forward

Are there any insights we'd like to take away from this conversation?

_____

_____

_____

_____

What would we like to do from here?

_____

_____

_____

_____

Apply self-discipline

Discipline is the difference between choosing what we want now and what we want most.

Abraham Lincoln

I often make myself porridge for breakfast. When I started, I never measured the ingredients and used to work out my ratio of oats to water by making the water level twice as high as the oats level.

For years, this method worked well, and I achieved consistently good results. Then, things changed.

A couple of my family members asked if I'd make them porridge too.

As a life-long student of the *Recipes are for Noobs[1] School of Cookery*, most of the time, I like to 'wing it' in the kitchen.

---

1   Noob is a colloquial term used to describe a rookie or newbie (ie. Noobie)

It keeps food interesting. There are plenty of times when my cooking turns out okay, but other times, well... not so much.

One thing is for sure: any dish I make is never the same twice.

So, back to the porridge situation.

For someone who likes to mix it up a little in the kitchen, I have surprisingly rigid requirements when it comes to porridge. I like it to be firm enough so that it holds its shape when you take a spoonful, but not so firm that its surface resembles the surface of the moon.

My rigid requirements and the additional porridge portions created an issue.

The bowl I used to make my porridge had curved sides, which meant that the diameter was much wider towards the top than the bottom. Therefore, for every centimetre I raised the waterline, the greater the actual volume of water I was adding. The same problem applied to the amount of oats.

As if that wasn't tricky enough, I then had to work out how long to cook it for.

Breakfast suddenly became way more complex. So much so, after many mornings of either stodgy or runny porridge, I decided to acknowledge defeat. I went to the back of the oats packet, followed its instructions and produced the perfect porridge.

Urgh! Don't you hate that?

This was one occasion where I had to acknowledge that my enthusiasm for 'winging it' wasn't serving me well. If you want a consistent result, discipline is important, even if it sometimes feels boring.

Curly questions to consider

Reflect in pairs

Which parts of this article resonated most with you?

_____

_____

_____

_____

Do you tend to prefer the creative approach to solutions or a more methodical one?

_____

_____

_____

_____

Respond as a team

What does 'winging it' look like in our environment?

_____

_____

_____

_____

When thinking about the way our team works, do we tend to 'wing it' or do we tend to be more disciplined?

_____

_____

_____

_____

The article talks about the *"Recipes are for Noobs"* School of Cookery. If our team opened a school, what would it be called?

E.g. The _____ School of _____

_____

_____

_____

_____

Why would it be called that?

_____

_____

_____

_____

Given what we do, how well does our approach work for us?

_____

_____

_____

_____

Review and look forward

What insights have we gained from this conversation?

_____

_____

_____

_____

Are there any aspects we've talked about that we'd like to explore further?

_____

_____

_____

_____

What should we do next?

_____

_____

_____

_____

Make
better choices

Value what we have

*Learn to appreciate what you have
before time makes you appreciate
what you had.*

Unknown

Often when we're dissatisfied with the way things are, our default response is to seek something new.

Let's face it - there's something quite seductive about having something new and different. It's a human characteristic that the entire retail sector relies on.

Unfortunately, in our desire for something bright and shiny, it's easy to overlook and undervalue the things we already have.

I was reminded of this recently.

My kitchen had an old sink that I wanted to replace. However, when I started looking for new sinks, I encountered a problem. My sink had been installed when dishwashers were less popular and so it had a drainage board that was much longer than those today. I therefore couldn't buy a new sink that was wide enough to cover the hole that the old sink would leave on my benchtop.

I realised that if I wanted a new sink, I also needed a new benchtop.

In moments, my planned investment of a couple of hundred dollars had blown up to not just one, but many thousands of dollars.

In my heart, I was inclined to go for the new benchtops with the shiny new sink. However, my head said to do one more check of the old sink to see how good I could make it look.

Actually, between you and I, what I really wanted to do was prove that the old sink was never going to look as good as a new one and therefore, justify the additional investment.

After watching a couple of DIY videos, I attacked the sink with steel wool, sandpaper, bicarbonate of soda and finally, metal polish.

I was amazed with the result. The old sink gleamed and looked almost new. This meant that when I compared what I now had to the outcome my thousands of dollars would have delivered, the value was much higher than if I had spent all of that money. I kept the sink, bought a new tap and redirected the money towards buying a new fridge.

But our tendency to gravitate towards something new is not limited to kitchens or buying the latest mobile device, gadget, or shoes. In business, we sometimes overlook the people and the expertise we have internally, in favour of bringing in new people (or things) from outside. Similarly, we buy a new system when what we really needed to do was make the old process better.

Going for something new is appealing because it feels like we need to think less. It can also feel like it's a faster way to achieve the outcome we want. However, like my sink, until you know what you already have and how valuable it is, how can you know what you really need?

Curly questions to consider

Reflect in pairs

Have you ever found yourself facing the equivalent of the sink dilemma?

_____

_____

_____

_____

Think about the last time you sought out something new. How much time did you spend valuing what you already had?

_____

_____

_____

_____

Respond as a team

Do we have more of a 'buy new' mindset or a 'use what we have' mindset?

_____

_____

_____

_____

Where does this mindset come from?

_____

_____

_____

_____

How does it influence the way we approach challenges?

_____

_____

_____

_____

What would happen if we adopted the opposite mindset?

_____

_____

_____

_____

Which would best support our success?

_____

_____

_____

_____

Is there anything we could do differently?

_____

_____

_____

_____

Review and look forward

What's one thing we could try?

_____

_____

_____

_____

What should we do next?

_____

_____

_____

_____

Set the right priorities

Desires dictate our priorities, priorities shape our choices, and choices determine our actions.

Dallin H. Oaks

In the late 1990s, the future of Port Melbourne Primary School was looking pretty grim. The State school's enrolments, along with its reputation, had been declining for many years. Port Melbourne Primary School was known locally for being kind of rough. A school to be avoided if you cared about your kid's education.

Families in the area who could afford it, sent their kids to privately run alternatives. This meant that the school's student population was skewed towards families who were socially and economically disadvantaged. It was a vicious cycle.

When the new principal arrived, the school had only 122 pupils.

Peter Martin was an experienced educator. He wasted no time trying to make improvements and ultimately, save the school from closure.

He brought in new, more experienced teachers. He repainted all the classrooms, transforming them from dowdy, tired cells to fresh places of learning. The old blackboards were removed, and modern whiteboards installed.

Peter waited with enthusiasm for the next year's enrolments to go up. But, much to his disappointment, very little changed. Still, despite all the efforts, no one wanted to send their kids to the local primary school.

It so happened that a major development involving many hundreds of houses was starting next to the school. Peter had an idea.

The fence around the school was two metres tall and made of battered chain metal. It made the school look more like a compound than a place of learning.

Peter approached the building developer and suggested that it would increase the attractiveness of the new suburb (and thus, house prices) if there was an attractive local primary school. He asked them to provide funding for a new fence, one that was only waist-high and made of more residential-style powder coated steel. The new fence made the school look more open and inviting. And, when the next year's enrolments came along, they increased significantly. They continued to do so from then on.

To create change, Peter needed to focus on what parents in the area could see and what they valued. It meant that the primary school needed to look like a good school, before it could become one.

During his time as principal, Peter Martin took the school from having 122 pupils to over 880.

I first met him when we were looking for a school for our daughter. Ever since then, this story has served as a powerful reminder of how important it is to focus on creating value for the people who create value for you.

Curly questions to consider

Reflect in pairs

Have you ever thought something was important, but no one else could see it?

_____

_____

_____

_____

Why might that have happened?

_____

_____

_____

_____

Respond as a team

In the article, what is meant by "focus on the things that create value for the people who create value for you"?

_____

_____

_____

_____

What does value look like in the context of our team?

_____

_____

_____

_____

Who do we aim to create value for?

_____

_____

_____

_____

How do they create value for us?

_____

_____

_____

_____

How clearly aligned are our priorities to the things that create value?

_____

_____

_____

_____

How does this impact our team's performance?

_____

_____

_____

_____

Review and look forward

Is this an area worth improving?

_____

_____

_____

_____

What should we do now?

_____

_____

_____

_____

Take the right risks

Courage is knowing what not to fear.

Plato

When my hometown was in lockdown due to the coronavirus pandemic, my daughter called me and asked if I would help her cut her hair.

But this wasn't your average haircut.

My daughter had decided that, as she had to stay home anyway, if ever she was going to shave her head, now was the time to do so. In ten short minutes, my daughter went from having hair that reached past her shoulders in length, to no hair at all.

But, let's bring this back to you.

Would you shave your head?

As you think about it, I'd like you to take a moment to reflect on what your brain did when I first asked the question.

For example, how soon after reading the question, did the answer come to you? Was it instant or did it take some time?

Was the answer a resounding 'yes' or 'no'? Or did you find your mind swinging backwards and forwards?

What factors did you consider? For example, how your boss would react? How you'd look with no hair? What other people might say? Were there any conditions to your answer? For instance, did you think "I would do it, if it were going to save my son's life or if you paid me a million dollars," or "I'd be willing to go shorter, but not do a complete shave?"

But why am I asking all these questions?

Well, reflecting on how we think helps us to be conscious of otherwise hidden factors that influence our decisions. In this simple example, the two influential factors at play were: the level of perceived risk associated with shaving your head, and your appetite for accepting those risks relative to the potential reward.

Let's say that you had little hair to start with and you thought that the shaved-head look would make you appear more attractive. You would probably have answered 'yes' because there was relatively little risk (i.e., you had hardly any hair anyway) and you expected the outcome to be an improvement.

But what if you were the news anchor for a leading television station? And what if you believed that shaving your head would be inconsistent with this role?

In this case, you may answer 'no' because you felt you'd be putting your career and your reputation at risk. And, you'd be expecting the outcome to place you in a worse position than today.

Every decision we make requires us to weigh up the risks.

When we're conscious of these mental processes it makes it easier to challenge our thoughts, beliefs and assumptions. This, in turn, leads us to better decisions.

Curly questions to consider

Reflect in pairs

What did you learn about your thinking when reading this article?

_____

_____

_____

_____

Think about a recent decision you made. What role did your perceived risks and rewards play in that decision?

_____

_____

_____

_____

Respond as a team

What kinds of risks do we consider when we're making decisions as a team?

_____

_____

_____

_____

How conscious are we of those risks?

_____

_____

_____

_____

On a scale from complete risk aversion to reckless risk taking, where does our collective appetite for risk sit?

_____

_____

_____

_____

How does our appetite for risk influence our decisions?

_____

_____

_____

_____

How could we better consider risks when making decisions?

_____

_____

_____

_____

What would need to change for that to occur?

_____

_____

_____

_____

Review and look forward

Which of those elements can we control?

_____

_____

_____

_____

What would we like to do next?

_____

_____

_____

_____

Embrace change

Seize opportunities

Life moves pretty fast. If you don't stop and look around once in a while, you could miss it.

Ferris Bueller – Ferris Bueller's Day Off

H ave you ever decided not to take an opportunity and found you regretted it later on?

A while ago I was travelling for work. It was the night before an off-site conference I was running with 150 people. A lot of conversations needed to be had and there was relatively little time to have them in.

The night before the conference, I stayed in my room. After months of preparation, all of the content was ready and so most of the work had been done. I knew that at this final stage, success would come down to three simple things:

Creating the right energy, obsessing about the logistics and being ready with 'Plan B'.

As I sat in my hotel room that evening, I wanted to go through each of these elements.

I ordered room service and when it arrived, I was excited to see a huge pile of crisp, beautifully formed chips on my plate. I love hot chips, but I only have them when I'm travelling for work.

These ones were perfect specimens. Crisp. Hot. Salty. Just what I needed.

I was famished.

I quickly ate nearly all of the chips then continued with my work. I finished an hour or so later and realised that I'd left a few of the chips on the plate. I remembered how delicious they had tasted and without thinking, I picked one up and ate it.

Erggh! It was cold, waxy and gross. Just thinking about it now gives me a nasty taste in my mouth. If only I had eaten them all while they were hot.

It was a small but important lesson.

Sometimes we forget that opportunities come with an expiry date. Therefore, when opportunities present themselves, we need to capture them in their entirety. Otherwise, we risk coming back later, only to find ourselves disappointed.

Curly questions to consider

Reflect in pairs

How would you define an opportunity?

_____

_____

_____

_____

What would such an opportunity look like if it were standing in front of you?

_____

_____

_____

_____

Respond as a team

If we were facing an opportunity, what characteristics would it have?

_____

_____

_____

_____

What's the difference between identifying and capturing opportunities?

_____

_____

_____

_____

How do we know if an opportunity is the right one for us?

_____

_____

_____

_____

What is the best opportunity we've captured recently?

_____

_____

_____

_____

What's an example of one that we missed?

_____

_____

_____

_____

Review and look forward

Is this conversation an opportunity to be captured?

_____

_____

_____

_____

What should we do about it?

_____

_____

_____

_____

Respond to the unexpected

When you get into trouble, always hold onto your oars.

My daughter

H ave you ever stood on the banks of a river and watched an experienced team of rowers pass by?

They make it look easy, don't they?

Of course, being part of a competitive rowing team is anything but easy, as my daughter discovered when she joined her high school team.

Prior to this, I'd never really had much to do with the sport. I'd always imagined that the most challenging element of rowing was getting everyone in the boat to move their oars together.

As it turned out, this assumption was reasonably correct. However, there was something even more basic than this. And, if a team failed to get it right, they would never, ever win a race.

What was this critical element?

The ability to stay in the boat.

You see, it turns out that the boat used by rowing teams is very unstable. That's because non-essential stabilisers are sacrificed in order to minimise the drag when the boat is cutting through the water.

It's kind of obvious, when you think about it.

When they are starting out, rowing teams frequently lose their rhythm and as a consequence, the oars of different rowers hit each other. When this happens, it causes turbulence both inside and outside the boat. This makes the boat rock from side to side.

It's in this moment that beginners do one of two things. Option one lands the team in the water and option two, enables the team to recover and continue rowing. Option one is a reaction and option two is a response.

When the boat starts to rock, the natural reaction for inexperienced rowers is to panic and when doing so, let go of their oars. When this happens, the oars become caught by the current of the water and smash against each other. This, of course, makes the boat rock even more. Eventually, one of the rowers loses their balance and the boat capsizes. This is option one.

The alternative response is for rowers to focus all their attention on holding onto their oars. This is option two and it does three things.

Firstly, it prevents the oars hitting each other, which causes further issues. Secondly, holding onto the oars means that the paddles can act as stabilisers, resting against the water's surface on either side of the boat.

And finally, holding the oars gives the rowers a job to do. Something to focus on when they are afraid and this helps them to feel more in control and thus, more calm.

Next time you find yourself in a wobbly situation and every element of your body is telling you to panic, remember:

Hold onto your oars and steer your way through it!

Curly questions to consider

Reflect in pairs

What do you think 'hold onto your oars' means in the last sentence?

_____

_____

_____

_____

If you were 'holding onto your oars' in the face of an unexpected event, what would you be doing?

_____

_____

_____

_____

Respond as a team

What's the difference between responding and reacting as a team?

_____

_____

_____

_____

Under what circumstances do we tend to react?

_____

_____

_____

_____

In what situations are we more likely to respond?

_____

_____

_____

_____

What causes us to behave differently?

_____

_____

_____

_____

Which approach serves us best?

_____

_____

_____

_____

How might we use the metaphor of 'holding onto our oars' to respond more effectively to the unexpected?

_____

_____

_____

_____

Review and look forward

Would we like to put this idea into practice?

_____

_____

_____

_____

If so, how could we do it?

_____

_____

_____

_____

Overcome adversity

Never give up on something that you can't go a day without thinking about.

Winston Churchill

In 2019, the World Mixed Curling Championships in Aberdeen were won by the Kosovo Curling Team.

The sport of curling has been around for centuries and is believed to have originated in Scotland from as far back as the 16th Century[7]. It is played by a team and involves sliding a rock down an ice-covered laneway, towards a target drawn on the ice. It's related to bowls or shuffleboard.

It would therefore be reasonable to assume that access to ice was a critical requirement to becoming a world champion curling team. However, as the Kosovo team discovered, this assumption was wrong.

You see, they came from a nation that had no ice rink. In fact, to train on ice, they would have had to travel over 1,000km (620 miles). Instead, they learnt the art of curling by sliding around a living room in socks.

Even days before the championships, the Kosovo team had never trained on actual ice. However, this was not where their challenges ended. They ran out of money, their visas to enter Scotland were delayed, and they arrived at the competition two hours after their first game was due to start.

The absence of an ice rink could have been a showstopper for the Kosovo Curling Team, but it wasn't. That's because instead of focusing on what they didn't have (an ice rink), the team focused on what they needed (that is, somewhere to train which was like ice and close by so they could practice often, together).

Sometimes all a big problem needs is a fresh perspective and the ability to look at the situation differently.

Curly questions to consider

Reflect in pairs

When have you found yourself facing an adverse situation?

_____

_____

_____

_____

What did it feel like?

_____

_____

_____

_____

Respond as a team

What is 'adversity'?

_____

_____

_____

_____

Where does it come from?

_____

_____

_____

_____

When has our team experienced an adverse situation that felt impossible?

_____

_____

_____

_____

How did we respond?

_____

_____

_____

_____

What positive aspects of our team help us in an adverse situation?

_____

_____

_____

_____

Are there aspects of our team that are unhelpful?

_____

_____

_____

_____

Review and look forward

Is this something we need to do something about?

_____

_____

_____

_____

What should we do?

_____

_____

_____

_____

How should we respond to the unexpected? How do we build trust? How do we engage our people? How do we think differently? Are we keeping our promises? How do we get on the same page? How do our... Could we make better choices? We challenge old habits? How do we connect better with each other? What does it mean to integrity? Do we learn from our mistakes? Is our strategy doing its job? How do we harness the power of self-discipline and purpose? Do we seize enough of our opportunities? Do we do the right things?

CONCLUSION

Over to you

You're off to great places, today is your day. Your mountain is waiting, so get on your way.

Dr Seuss

When writing this book, I wanted to leave you satisfied with what you'd learnt and thinking differently about your team and the conversations that it has. I also wanted to leave you hopeful and optimistic about the future, and feeling more in control. Finally, I wanted to plant a seed of curiosity that left you excited by the possibilities of a simple idea and keen to discover more.

So, while we've reached the end of the book, I hope that you'll feel it's more of a beginning.

But before we close, let's review some of the key ideas we've talked about.

The story so far

We've learnt that important jobs get disrupted, and that not all disruption is the same.

We've also discovered that disruption has both a visible and a hidden side and we can use the Wheel of Disruption to analyse and talk about what has happened. Used with your team, the Wheel of Disruption will allow a human-centered discussion of individual perspectives, interpretations, and emotional responses to a disrupted situation.

Towards the end of Part 1, we met the creatures of comfort and the critters of chaos. Use this language in your team. It will enable people to acknowledge when they are caught in the Discomfort Dilemma, stand back from it, and then deal with it differently.

In Part 2, we looked at two kinds of conversations that can happen when your team is in its discomfort zone. Chaotic Conversations occur when a situation is not straightforward and we don't change our thinking and approach to match it. The consequences leave your team feeling frustrated, confused and exhausted. This increases the risk of a compromised outcome.

The alternative is to have a Curly Conversation. These happen by design and work with the rugged terrain of a disrupted environment, rather than trying to fight against it. Curly Conversations leave your team feeling focused, confident and energised.

If you want to make Curly Conversations a standard practice within your team, you now have a three-stage roadmap that shows how to get there. Start with Discovery, move on to Exploration and then pursue Mastery. We also talked about the three strands of success. Calm the critters, create connections and build cognitive competence. These important principles underlie every Curly Conversation and will enable your team to make progress, despite uncertainty.

In Parts 3 and 4, the baton was handed over to you and your team to have your own Curly Conversations.

Different readers use *Curly Conversations for teams* in different ways. Whether you've already had the 15 conversations within your team, or you're about to start, I hope you find them easy to use, insightful and energising.

Let's continue the conversation

I have to be honest with you. As a passionate Curly Converser, it has taken considerable restraint for me to stop here.

I'm bursting to share things like: how a Curly Conversation works from the inside; how you can invite people to step into the conversation; how to design the right questions when you are facing a particularly *curly* conundrum.

And then, there are other important questions to answer like:

- Why is the first half of a Curly Conversation so much harder than the second half?

- How do you work out what kind of a conundrum you are dealing with and what that means for your team?

- How do you build momentum, even when you only have a short amount of time?

I've stopped here because learning a new skill (and letting go of an old one) can be hard to do. This is particularly so when we are talking about the collective capability of a team.

If you'd like to learn more, let's continue the conversation.

Sign up for my *Curly, Calm and Curious* blog, drop me an email at **hello@katechristiansen.com.au** or visit **www.curlyconversations.com**

Thanks for reading and let's keep talking.

Acknowledgement

As with any book, this one would not have been possible without the support and generosity of many people around me. I am immensely grateful to my dear friend Gabrielle for her tough love, encouragement and editorial advice. Thank you also to my generous previewers who so willingly gave their time and provided such invaluable feedback. I am indebted to: Lisa O'Neill who saw this possibility long before I did; Kate Billing for setting the challenge that made it happen; and to Dr Kelly Windle for our many thought-provoking and energising conversations.

And as always, thank you to my beautiful family for your enduring humour, love and encouragement.

Endnotes

1. This story was first told on ABC radio Melbourne and you can hear the original recording here. Mornings with Sammy J - 'You Flamin' Galah!' File under: One of the Greatest Rescues of All-Time - Breakfast - ABC Radio. ABC Radio, Australian Broadcasting Commission, 27 Aug. 2020, https://www.abc.net.au/radio/melbourne/programs/breakfast/james-mitchell-galah-rescue/12600738.

2. Coleman, A. *A Dictionary of Psychology (3 ed.)*. Oxford University Press. 2009. For a brief summary of the Yerkes-Dodson Law.

3. "CONVERSATION | Meaning in the Cambridge English Dictionary." Cambridge Dictionary | English Dictionary, Translations & Thesaurus, Cambridge Press, https://dictionary.cambridge.org/dictionary/english/conversation. Accessed 18 Dec. 2020.

4. "CHAT | Meaning in the Cambridge English Dictionary." Cambridge Dictionary | English Dictionary, Translations & Thesaurus, https://dictionary.cambridge.org/dictionary/english/chat. Accessed 18 Dec. 2020.

5. Parker, M. *Humble PI: When Math Goes Wrong in the Real Word*. Illustrated, Riverhead Books, 2020.

6. Bridges, Business Consulting. "Strategy Implementation Findings." Annual Survey Report, 2012.

7. The sport of Curling originated in Scotland. Written references date back as far as 1541. Learn more at "History of the Game - Scottish Curling." Wayback Machine, https://web.archive.org/web/20180215083915/http://www.scottishcurling.org/curling-history/history-of-the-game/. Accessed 18 Dec. 2020.

www.ingramcontent.com/pod-product-compliance
Lightning Source LLC
Chambersburg PA
CBHW071226210326
41597CB00016B/1967